Exclusive O

As our valued reader, your purchase of this book includes access to exclusive online resources designed to enhance your learning experience. These resources can be downloaded from our website, www.vibrantpublishers.com, and are created to help you apply Product Management concepts effectively.

Online resources for this book include the following essential templates:

- Company strategy: SWOT analysis
- 5C analysis
- Porter's 5 forces
- Market analysis: Business model canvas
- PESTLE analysis
- BCG Growth Market Share Metrics/Matrix
- Pragmatic marketing
- TAM/SAM/SOM analysis
- Kano Model
- Sample PRD format

Why these online resources are valuable:

- **Practical application:** The ready-to-use templates simplify complex product management processes.
- **Step-by-step guidance:** They enable a clear understanding of concepts, efficient implementation of techniques, and skill refinement.
- **Enhanced learning experience:** They will help you apply the concepts learning in the book in real-world scenarios.

How to access your online resources:

1. **Visit the website:** Go to www.vibrantpublishers.com
2. **Find your book:** Navigate to the book's product page via the "Shop" menu or by searching for the book title in the search bar.
3. **Request the resources:** Scroll down to the «Request Sample Book/Online Resource» section.
4. **Enter your details:** Enter your preferred email ID and select "Online Resource" as the resource type. Lastly, select "user type" and submit the request.
5. **Check your inbox:** The resources will be delivered directly to your email.

Alternatively, for quick access: simply scan the QR code below to go directly to the product page and request the online resources by filling in the required details.

bit.ly/pm-slm

Happy learning!

SELF-LEARNING MANAGEMENT SERIES

PRODUCT MANAGEMENT ESSENTIALS
YOU ALWAYS WANTED TO KNOW

A practical guide to becoming
a top-tier product manager

CHINTAN UDESHI

PRODUCT MANAGEMENT ESSENTIALS YOU ALWAYS WANTED TO KNOW

First Edition

Copyright © 2025, by Vibrant Publishers LLC, USA. All rights reserved. No part of this publication may be reproduced or distributed in any form or by any means, or stored in a database or retrieval system, without the prior permission of the publisher.

Published by Vibrant Publishers LLC, USA, www.vibrantpublishers.com

Paperback ISBN 13: 978-1-63651-479-6
Ebook ISBN 13: 978-1-63651-480-2
Hardback ISBN 13: 978-1-63651-481-9

Library of Congress Control Number: 2025935451

This publication is designed to provide accurate and authoritative information in regard to the subject matter covered. The Author has made every effort in the preparation of this book to ensure the accuracy of the information. However, information in this book is sold without warranty either expressed or implied. The Author or the Publisher will not be liable for any damages caused or alleged to be caused either directly or indirectly by this book.

All trademarks and registered trademarks mentioned in this publication are the property of their respective owners. These trademarks are used for editorial and educational purposes only, without intent to infringe upon any trademark rights. This publication is independent and has not been authorized, endorsed, or approved by any trademark owner.

Vibrant Publishers' books are available at special quantity discount for sales promotions, or for use in corporate training programs. For more information please write to bulkorders@vibrantpublishers.com

Please email feedback / corrections (technical, grammatical or spelling) to spellerrors@vibrantpublishers.com

Vibrant publishes in a variety of print and electronic formats and by print-on-demand. Some material included with standard print versions of this book may not be included in e-books or in print-on-demand. To access the complete catalogue of Vibrant Publishers, visit www.vibrantpublishers.com

SELF-LEARNING MANAGEMENT SERIES

TITLE	PAPERBACK* ISBN

BUSINESS AND ENTREPRENEURSHIP

BUSINESS COMMUNICATION ESSENTIALS	9781636511634
BUSINESS ETHICS ESSENTIALS	9781636513324
BUSINESS LAW ESSENTIALS	9781636511702
BUSINESS PLAN ESSENTIALS	9781636511214
BUSINESS STRATEGY ESSENTIALS	9781949395778
ENTREPRENEURSHIP ESSENTIALS	9781636511603
INTERNATIONAL BUSINESS ESSENTIALS	9781636513294
PRINCIPLES OF MANAGEMENT ESSENTIALS	9781636511542

COMPUTER SCIENCE AND TECHNOLOGY

BLOCKCHAIN ESSENTIALS	9781636513003
MACHINE LEARNING ESSENTIALS	9781636513775
PYTHON ESSENTIALS	9781636512938

DATA SCIENCE FOR BUSINESS

BUSINESS INTELLIGENCE ESSENTIALS	9781636513362
DATA ANALYTICS ESSENTIALS	9781636511184

FINANCIAL LITERACY AND ECONOMICS

COST ACCOUNTING & MANAGEMENT ESSENTIALS	9781636511030
FINANCIAL ACCOUNTING ESSENTIALS	9781636510972
FINANCIAL MANAGEMENT ESSENTIALS	9781636511009
MACROECONOMICS ESSENTIALS	9781636511818
MICROECONOMICS ESSENTIALS	9781636511153
PERSONAL FINANCE ESSENTIALS	9781636511849
PRINCIPLES OF ECONOMICS ESSENTIALS	9781636512334

*Also available in Hardback & Ebook formats

SELF-LEARNING MANAGEMENT SERIES

TITLE	PAPERBACK* ISBN
HR, DIVERSITY, AND ORGANIZATIONAL SUCCESS	
DIVERSITY, EQUITY, AND INCLUSION ESSENTIALS	9781636512976
DIVERSITY IN THE WORKPLACE ESSENTIALS	9781636511122
HR ANALYTICS ESSENTIALS	9781636510347
HUMAN RESOURCE MANAGEMENT ESSENTIALS	9781949395839
ORGANIZATIONAL BEHAVIOR ESSENTIALS	9781636512303
ORGANIZATIONAL DEVELOPMENT ESSENTIALS	9781636511481
LEADERSHIP AND PERSONAL DEVELOPMENT	
DECISION MAKING ESSENTIALS	9781636510026
INDIA'S ROAD TO TRANSFORMATION: WHY LEADERSHIP MATTERS	9781636512273
LEADERSHIP ESSENTIALS	9781636510316
TIME MANAGEMENT ESSENTIALS	9781636511665
MODERN MARKETING AND SALES	
CONSUMER BEHAVIOR ESSENTIALS	9781636513263
DIGITAL MARKETING ESSENTIALS	9781949395747
MARKETING MANAGEMENT ESSENTIALS	9781636511788
MARKET RESEARCH ESSENTIALS	9781636513744
SALES MANAGEMENT ESSENTIALS	9781636510743
SERVICES MARKETING ESSENTIALS	9781636511733
SOCIAL MEDIA MARKETING ESSENTIALS	9781636512181

*Also available in Hardback & Ebook formats

SELF-LEARNING MANAGEMENT SERIES

TITLE	PAPERBACK* ISBN
OPERATIONS MANAGEMENT	
AGILE ESSENTIALS	9781636510057
OPERATIONS & SUPPLY CHAIN MANAGEMENT ESSENTIALS	9781949395242
PROJECT MANAGEMENT ESSENTIALS	9781636510712
STAKEHOLDER ENGAGEMENT ESSENTIALS	9781636511511
CURRENT AFFAIRS	
DIGITAL SHOCK	9781636513805

*Also available in Hardback & Ebook formats

Table of Contents

1 Introduction to Product Management — 1

- 1.1 Why Do Organizations Need Product Managers? 2
- 1.2 A Product Manager's Goals and Responsibilities 4
- 1.3 A Day In the Life of A Product Manager 9
- 1.4 How are Product Managers Different from Project Managers, Program Managers, and Scrum Masters 12
- Chapter Summary 15
- Quiz 16

2 Identifying Product Opportunities — 19

- 2.1 Market Analysis and Understanding Customers' Needs 20
- 2.3 Competition 22
- 2.4 Segmentation, Targeting, and Positioning (STP) 22
- 2.5 Vision → Strategy 26
- 2.6 User and Buyer Personas 29
- 2.7 Business Model Canvas 30
- 2.8 Users' Group and Customer Interactions 32
- Chapter Summary 33
- Quiz 34

3 Converting Strategy into a Product — 37

- 3.1 Strategy → Roadmap 38
- 3.2 Feature Prioritization 40
- 3.3 Crafting Product Specifications/Requirements 50
- 3.4 Building the Product - Waterfall vs Agile 54
- 3.5 Building an MVP → Launching the POC/Private Preview 57
- 3.6 Product Pricing 59
- 3.7 Launching the Product 60
- Chapter Summary 61
- Quiz 62

4 Product Messaging and Launching the Product — 65

- 4.1 Developing a Go-To-Market (GTM) Strategy — 66
- 4.2 Product Positioning — 69
- 4.3 Understanding Product Buying Cycle/Purchase Funnel — 71
- 4.4 Launch Plan — 73
- 4.5 Collateral Building — 77
- 4.6 Announcement and PR — 79
- 4.7 Digital and Social Media Marketing — 82
- 4.8 Measuring GTM Success — 84
- 4.9 Post-Launch Activities — 87
- Chapter Summary — 90
- Quiz — 91

5 After the First Product Launch — 95

- 5.1 Measuring Success — 96
- 5.2 Customer Feedback Loop — 99
- 5.3 Understanding the Product Lifecycle — 102
- 5.4 Win-Loss Analysis and Funnel Analysis — 106
- 5.5 Portfolio Planning — 110
- 5.6 Lifetime Value of the Customer — 112
- Chapter Summary — 117
- Quiz — 118

6 Skills Needed to Become A Top-Tier Product Manager — 121

- 6.1 Customer Empathy — 122
- 6.2 Communication — 123
- 6.3 Tech/Domain Knowledge — 125
- 6.4 Leading Without Authority — 127
- 6.5 Business Acumen — 130
- 6.6 Relationship Management — 132
- 6.7 Negotiation — 133
- 6.8 Attention to Details — 134
- 6.9 Data Analysis — 135
- Chapter Summary — 137
- Quiz — 138

7 Product Management Specializations — 141
7.1 B2B vs. B2C Product Management   142
7.2 Generalist PM vs. Growth PM vs. Platform PM   145
7.3 Inbound vs. Outbound Product Management   148
Chapter Summary   153
Quiz   154

8 Commonly Used Product Management Frameworks — 157
8.1 SWOT Analysis   158
8.2 5C Analysis   159
8.3 Porter's Five Forces   161
8.4 Cluster Analysis   163
8.5 Conjoint Analysis   165
8.6 4P Analysis   168
8.7 Customer Purchases Decision Framework   170
8.8 Business Model Canvas   171
8.9 PESTLE Analysis   174
8.10 BCG Growth Market Share Matrix   177
8.11 Pricing Decisions   179
8.12 Build, Partner, Buy Analysis   185
8.13 Pragmatic Marketing Framework   186
8.14 TAM/SAM/SOM Analysis   187
8.15 Kano Model   189
8.16 Sample PRD Format   191
Chapter Summary   194
Quiz   196

9 How to Get Into Product Management — 199
9.1 Transitioning From Different Roles to the PM role   200
9.2 Hiring and Interview Process   203
9.3 Career Paths in Product Management   207
9.4 Do You Need An MBA to Become A Successful PM?   208
Chapter Summary   211
Quiz   212

10 Cracking the PM Interview: Types of Questions and Tips 215

10.1 What Tech Companies Look for in PM - Amazon, Microsoft, Apple, and Facebook 216
10.2 Types of Interview Questions 218
10.3 Importance of Networking and Mentorship 225
Chapter Summary 226
Quiz 227

Bibliography 230

Further Learning 232

About the Author

Chintan Udeshi has over 15 years of experience working in the tech industry where he has held various roles including software engineer, program manager, product marketing manager, and product manager. As a seasoned professional, Chintan is passionate about building products that make customer's lives easy and he has accomplished this both as an engineer and as a product manager. Chintan started his career as an engineer in India and shortly after that, he moved to the USA to pursue a Masters degree in Computer Science. After finishing school, he worked as an engineer for a few years before deciding to go back to school to pursue an MBA.

After completing an MBA, he has worked for 7+ years as a product manager including experience in big companies and startups, focusing on cloud technologies, cybersecurity, and Artificial Intelligence (AI) products. Currently, Chintan is working as a Principal Product Manager in the tech industry, where he is leading the network security products that allow customers to protect applications running on public and private clouds as well as AI applications.

Since transitioning to a product role, Chintan has mentored 100+ candidates interested in transitioning to the product manager role. With this book, he is covering everything he has learned about the product manager role, how to transition to the product manager role and once you become a product manager, how to succeed in the role.

What Experts Say About This Book!

This book does a great job of balancing breadth and real-world relevance. It speaks directly to early-career professionals and aspiring PMs, demystifying not just the 'what' but the 'why' behind key product management practices. What stands out is how it connects frameworks, customer centricity, and practical tools like MVP validation into one coherent flow. A solid foundation for anyone stepping into the PM world.

– Dinker Charak, Author,
Creating Products That Matter

Product Management Essentials is an excellent book for anyone looking for a holistic view of Product Management. I am very impressed with the wide array of concepts covered, the well-structured format of the book, and the clarity with which the concepts have been presented, often with practical examples. I would also highly recommend it to early-stage PMs to keep them grounded in the basics of Product Management, even as their everyday work hustle overwhelms them. Many of the tools that Chintan has included should come across as a refreshing reminder to PMs and help them get more effective in their role.

– Raghu Ramanujam, Senior Director,
Product Management, Flipkart

I was fortunate enough to review Chintan's book and discovered that its value extends far beyond the formal education a Product Manager needs. I believe this book has the potential to provide readers with lasting knowledge that can help them enter Product Management and increase their earning potential.

– Swagat Appasaheb Irsale, Former Product Leader at Phenom

Preface

What does the product manager role entail? How do I transition to a product manager role? How do I crack the product manager interview? And do I need an MBA to become a product manager? These are some of the questions that I get all the time when I am mentoring aspiring product managers.

When I started my career as an engineer, I had absolutely no idea what the product manager role was and never even heard of that role. But as I started understanding how different departments within the organization come together to bring the product to the market, I started to understand the strategic importance of the product manager role.

Initially, I was fascinated by the cross-functional aspect of the product manager role and how they work across different departments to bring the product to the market and then iteratively improve the product. As I started to peel the onion, I realized that the role was much more than that. The role entails a detailed understanding of the industry, different players in the market, and most importantly, a thorough understanding of the customer journey and pain points. Once these details are well understood, product managers need to come up with a strategy to bring the product to the market that will solve the customer's critical problems and enable the company to generate revenue and gain the market in the long run. While I quickly realized that I wanted to become a product manager, understanding and acquiring the skills needed to become a product manager took considerable time and effort.

After transitioning to a PM role and working as a product manager for 7+ years in the tech industry, including tenure at big companies and startups, I understand a lot more about the product manager role than I did when I started my career. I have a much better understanding of the role, responsibilities, and what it takes to succeed as a PM, both in the big organizations and in the startup world. Along the way, I received guidance and mentorship from lots of people in the industry.

As I started gaining experience in the product manager role, I started guiding candidates who wanted to take a similar journey and transition to the product manager role. In the past 5 years, I have mentored 100+ candidates who are interested in transitioning to the product manager role. With this book, my attempt is to cover everything I have learned about the product manager role, how to make the transition to it, and once you become a product manager, how to succeed in the role.

Introduction to the Book

In the fast-moving and technologically advancing world, companies need to continuously evolve to meet and exceed expectations of their customers. Companies need to bring the new products and offerings to the market to meet and exceed customer needs and solve the important problems for the customers and make their life easy. To ensure the product meets and exceeds the customer expectation and businesses remain competitive, the role of the product manager has become crucial in an organization as it involves deeply understanding the customer preferences and the industry in general and then, coming up with a strategy to solve the customer problems in a differentiated way to ensure it delights the customers. The product manager role sits at an intersection of technology, marketing and sales and hence, product managers need to work cross-functionality across different departments to bring the products into the market.

Product Management Essentials You Always Wanted to Know (*Product Management Essentials*) is a comprehensive and easily understandable guide for anyone who wants to learn about the product manager role, how to become a product manager for the first time and once you are in the PM role, how to succeed as a product manager in large organizations as well as startups.

The book is useful for aspiring product managers or early career product managers who know nothing about the product management role but want to learn more about the role including goals and responsibilities, day in the life of the product manager. It also covers the cross-functional nature of the product manager role and how PMs work cross-functionally across different departments to bring products into the market.

The author aims to debunk the long-standing myth that product management is too hard to break into, and only a very few lucky ones eventually become PM. From his personal experiences, the author understands that anyone, irrespective of their current jobs or professions, can successfully become a product manager if they seriously prepare for it. What separates *Product Management Essentials* from other PM books out there is that it is easy to understand, and provides practical and hands-on approaches that so that even the novice in the field can easily understand and apply them in the real world situations.

By reading this book, the reader will gain an understanding of the following topics:

- Product manager roles and responsibilities and day in the life of product manager

- How to identify product opportunities and work cross-functionally across different departments to launch the product into the market.

- Frameworks that are commonly used by the product managers to make the strategic decisions for the product as well as overall organization.

- Product management specializations and how to become top 10% of product manager

- How to get into the product management role and cracking the PM interviews

Who Can Benefit From This Book?

- Students and early career professionals interested in understanding what a career in product management entails

- Aspiring product managers including professionals and students, especially those pursuing a business degree

- Professionals with limited exposure to the product manager role but those who want a deeper understanding of their product management counterparts

- Anyone with a desire to know more about the product management field, and its relevance in today's world

How to Use This Book

This book, can be used as a reference guide to understanding the role and relevance of the product management role in today's fast-evolving world.

Whether you are using it as a resource to brilliantly pass your Product Management certification exams, improve your existing knowledge in product management, or utilize it as teaching material in your management classes, this book simplifies the critical concepts and provides practical and hands-on approaches to apply the knowledge in real-world scenarios. about product management. Depending on your learning goals and level of understanding of the product manager role, you may want to pay extra attention to the appropriate sections of the book.

For example:

1. If you're just starting to learn about product management, start with chapter 1 and read the book straight through to the end.
2. If you want to learn about how product managers identify product opportunities, build strategy, and work cross-functionally to bring products to the market, check out the information in chapters 2 and 3.
3. If you want to learn about the outbound aspect of the product manager role and how the product manager iteratively improves the product, check out the information in chapters 4 and 5.
4. If you want to learn about frameworks that product managers use on a regular basis to make the right decisions, check out the information in Chapter 8.

5. If you want to learn about how to get into the product manager role and crack the interview, check out the information in chapters 9 and 10.
6. All the chapters have high-resolution graphics that advance the book's usefulness, and there are helpful quizzes at the end of each chapter for readers to test themselves on the skill or knowledge they have just acquired in the chapter.

Chapter 1
Introduction to Product Management

Key Learning Objectives
- The need for product managers in organizations
- A product manager's goals and responsibilities
- Difference between a product manager, a project manager, a program manager, and a scrum master

It is an undeniable fact that the success of any company depends largely on the quality and usefulness of its products. This explains why medium and large-sized enterprises dedicate a separate department called product management. It is the core responsibility of product managers to deliver a winning product to their organizations. The role of a product manager involves handling all activities within a company or organization that are concerned with planning, developing, managing, and launching a product. In this chapter, we will learn all about the core responsibilities of product managers.

1.1 Why Do Organizations Need Product Managers?

Companies are built to solve consumers' pain points. To accomplish this, they have to create products, whether tangible (physical goods) or intangible (services). Successful products make customers happy, and customers in turn reward the companies that make these products with revenue, and possibly long-term loyalty. This is something every company dreams of because this will translate into stable revenue, and, of course, profitability for the company in the long run. Hence, companies need product managers to help them launch and manage amazing products that are a good market fit and useful for end customers.

Figure 1.1 Functions of a product manager

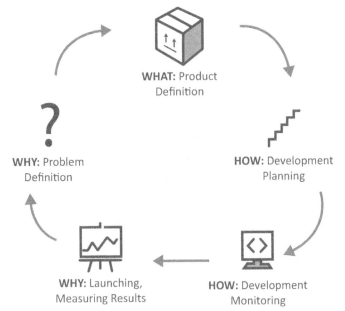

Source: Asano, Jacqueline Yumi. "Product Managers: What They Do and Why We Need Them." *Building Nubank* (blog), August 21, 2020. https://medium.com.

Figure 1.1 reveals the essential functions product managers carry out in a company. These functions provide decisive answers to the questions, *Why, what,* and *how*? The loop in Figure 1.1 starts with problem definition, followed by product definition, development planning and monitoring, and launching and measuring results. Let's understand each of these functions and questions in detail:

- **Problem definition:** Answering the *Why* questions i.e. **Why** do we need to produce a new product? What problem will it solve for our current and prospective customers?

- **Product definition:** Answering the *What* questions i.e. **What** kind of product do we need to develop? What existing or new features should it have?

- **Development planning and monitoring:** Answering the *How* questions i.e.
  How are we going to plan and develop this product? How are we going to launch it so that people who want it can have access to it?

- **Launching and measuring results**
  Is the launch and product adoption meeting the expectations? What changes do we need to make to ensure the product is widely adopted in the market?

Sometimes, it takes just a few months to create an entirely new product from scratch. For example, software, food, or paper products. In contrast, pharmaceutical, aviation, or space-related products may take product managers anywhere between five to ten years to be fully ready for deployment. Organizations need product managers to be involved right from the beginning, i.e. the conceptualizing stage, followed by planning, to launching the product. Once the product is launched, product managers are expected to understand the market traction and iteratively improve the product.

1.2 A Product Manager's Goals and Responsibilities

While launching a successful product sounds straightforward in theory, product managers have to manage lots of responsibilities to ensure the product solves the customers' problems and is adopted by the customers. The organization that produces such a successful product can ultimately cash in on its success for a long time. Figure 1.2 highlights the various roles and responsibilities of a product manager to make a product successful. The orange bar in the figure refers to different areas of PM work and the blue ones refer to tasks/responsibilities PMs need to do to complete that work. For example, to plan strategy for the product (as denoted by the second orange bar), PMs need to perform the following tasks: market definition, distribution strategy, product portfolio, and product roadmap (as denoted by the blue boxes in that column).

More information about each of the segments in this image is discussed in chapters seven and eight.

Figure 1.2 Roles and responsibilities of a product manager

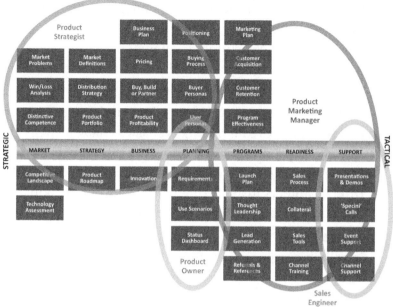

Source: Pragmatic Institute - Resources. "The Strategic Role of Product Management." Accessed November 21, 2024. https://www.pragmaticinstitute.com.

The goals and responsibilities of product managers widely vary depending on whether they are championing a new product or refining an existing one. Additionally, the product manager's role also varies from company to company and might be determined based on whether the product manager is working in a big company or a startup. As indicated in Figure 1.2, product managers can perform these four unique roles while overseeing a product's lifecycle:

- **Product strategist:** The main goal of a product strategist is to identify new opportunities in line with the organization's visions/missions, assess the performance of the organization's existing or new products, and develop a long-term, strategic business plan for the organization's future product lines.

- **Product owner:** A product owner manages and optimizes product backlog to maximize the product's value through a well-structured development management process, ensuring that the final product meets the requirements set by the stakeholders and customers.

- **Product marketing manager:** A product marketing manager handles the entire marketing and sales enablement aspect of a product, from owning the messaging, and product positioning, and gathering useful feedback/data from customers to analyzing them to advance product development and marketing efforts.

- **Sales engineer:** Sales engineers normally specialize in selling companies' products to the end customer. They are required to have a thorough knowledge of the products to explain the usefulness or benefits of their products and services to prospective buyers/customers. They may be required to do some demos or presentations and/or offer technical support to prospective customers.

In general, the product goes through various stages of a life cycle, commonly referred to as Product Life Cycle Management (PLM). Product managers are required to create a high-value product for the organization irrespective of the current stage of the product. The stages of the product life cycle include:

1. **Concept:** A product concept is the first stage in the product life cycle. It involves brainstorming detailed descriptions of the product, such as what kind of product to build, what features it will have, and what usefulness it will serve in order to help customers solve their pressing pain points or problems. Due to the high

failure rate of new products, it is extremely important to focus on product conception and talk to as many potential customers as possible to check the viability of the product.

> **FUN FACT**
>
> According to Clayton Christensen, a professor at Harvard Business School, there are about 30,000 new products developed every single year, but 95% of them miss the mark or fail.[1]

2. **Prototype:** Organizations don't normally rush into investing large proportions of time and money into a new product. Instead, product managers identify the most important features to validate the feasibility of the product and work with the engineering team to build a prototype, a mock-up, or a miniature version of the product. For intangible products like software, the first version is pretty much a Proof of Concept (PoC) of the product, consisting of the necessary features to guarantee the product works as envisaged. It is more cost-effective to produce a prototype than to make the entire product up front. After building the PoC/prototype, useful feedback can be obtained from the customers/stakeholders and utilized in building the right end product for the customers.

3. **Development:** After gathering feedback from the customers in the prototype phase, the product managers will then proceed to the next stage, which is

---

[1] Massachusetts Institute of Technology (2024). *Why 95% of new products miss the mark (and how yours can avoid the same fate).* Retrieved from https://professionalprograms.mit.edu

identifying the features that are needed for the initial version of the product. At this point, product managers will discuss how the product's prioritized features meet consumers' needs based on the initial analysis of the industry trends and customer feedback. They will need to investigate how their new product will fare against its competitors already available in the market so as to increase its chance of success.

4. **Launch:** Once the features are finalized for version one (v1) of the product, and the engineering team gets busy building v1 of the product, the product manager works with the other departments to plan the launch/announcement for the new product to their customers. In this stage, product managers typically work with the Product Marketing team to create the messaging for the product to ensure the product launch showcases a unique value proposition and differentiation of the product.

5. **Manufacture (applies to hardware products):** The process of manufacturing hardware products can take anywhere from a few days to a few months depending on a number of factors such as the product types, their sizes, how complex they are, and the resources that the manufacturers have at their disposal.

Product managers need to ensure that the product is produced strictly in accordance with the designed specifications. After that, product managers also need to ensure that the product passes through the appropriate quality control testing.[2]

- **Product consumption:** Once the product is launched, product managers work closely with their

---

[2]. Bland, D.J. Osterwalder, A. (2019). Testing Business Ideas: A Field Guide for Rapid Experimentation. London: Wiley, p. 34.

organizations' customer service centers to learn a lot about consumers' feedback. Are customers enjoying the product? Are their pain points being taken care of by the product? What else can the organization do to help customers derive satisfaction from using it? What improvements do the customers expect the organization to make on the second version of the product? These are some of the questions a product manager must look into and plan on iteratively improving the product.

- **Services:** Some products require post-sale services, and product managers will liaise with their companies' service departments to ensure that customers find the product very useful. In principle, many companies have a large 'Customer Success' department to ensure customers are successfully using the product.

After the launch of the product, it is possible to discover that a product (software, for example) may not be easy to use, and doesn't fully work in the customer's environment. This calls for the iterative improvement of the product since the first launched version (1.0) of software rarely satisfies all the customers' needs and requires continuous improvements and additional functionality to make it successful.

1.3 A Day In the Life of A Product Manager

To make sure the product is successfully launched and adopted by the customers, product managers need to handle the following day-to-day responsibilities:

1. **Connecting and communicating:** One of the core responsibilities of product managers is to liaise and communicate with all the stakeholders linked with bringing a product to life. Product managers proactively communicate with external stakeholders

such as customers, analysts, partners, suppliers, third-party research firms, etc. Similarly, they hold productive conversations with internal stakeholders from different departments including engineering, sales, design, marketing, legal teams, and so on.

Figure 1.3 The interrelationship between the product managers and other teams

Source: Adapted from "The product manager role, responsibilities, and skills", n.d. https://business.adobe.com

Figure 1.3 clearly reveals how product managers work across the aisle, liaising with professionals from other departments, and negotiating with developers, the engineering staff, sales and marketing teams, business managers, and legal teams to ensure that they create a useful product that solves the customer problem and aligns with their organizations' long-term goals.

2. **Learning and analyzing:** Since product managers oversee a product's lifecycle that requires significant contributions from experts in other departments, it is indispensable for product managers to embody a spirit of learning. They also need to keep an eye on the broader industry and competitors to identify new opportunities to improve the product. Not only that, they must consistently analyze the information/data and utilize it effectively to build the right product for the customers.

3. **Making decisions and documenting:** Product managers make vital decisions that are aligned with their organizations' product visions, properly document them for future reference, and refine them as needed during a product's lifecycle management (PLM).

Product managers carry out these important activities to move the product in the right direction:

- **Meetings:** Product managers actively participate in both regular and irregular meetings. In addition to internal meetings, they also find time to attend external meetings with customers, focus groups, and research companies.
- **Research:** Product managers undertake a lot of research geared towards product development, such as identifying consumers' pain points and unfulfilled needs, validating products' features and ideas, discovering users' behaviors and motivations, and identifying struggling features and improving them. These responsibilities are necessary to ensure the product's success.

- **Strategic planning:** Moreover, product managers plan a long-term strategy for the product. In most cases, product managers also participate in product messaging and collaborate with the customer service team to obtain vital feedback about the product. Such feedback can be utilized in refining the product so that users can derive maximum satisfaction from it.[3]

> Watch this video titled "Day in the Life of a Product Manager" to discover what it means to be a product manager!
>
> *https://www.youtube.com/watch?v=22aqrGizK6o*
>
> (Link also available in Online Resources)
>
> **Source:** *Stanford (University) Online*

1.4 How are Product Managers Different from Project Managers, Program Managers, and Scrum Masters

Much of what product managers do is highlighted in sections 1.1, 1.2, and 1.3. The role of a product manager is often confused with other roles such as scrum master, program manager, and project manager. However, there are striking differences between a product manager, project manager, and scrum master.

1.4.1 Who is a scrum master?

A scrum master's primary responsibility is to ensure that every team connected to a project performs their assigned

---

[3]. LeMay, M. (2017). Product Management in Practice: A Real-World Guide to the Key Connective Role of the 21st Century. Sebastopol, CA: O'Reilly Media, p. 55.

duties in accordance with the scrum principles. Scrum principles foster self-organization, streamlined collaboration, iterative development, and value-based process control. In practice, the scrum team comprises scrum masters, product owners or managers, and the development team. Even though scrum masters do not necessarily have the power to make strategic decisions touching product planning, designing, and development, they act as facilitators, creating a good atmosphere for smooth communication and cooperation among all the teams.

When required, scrum masters can train team members in relation to scrum practices and organize meetings for them. The primary role of a scrum master is to streamline the product management procedure by ensuring everyone is doing what they should be doing within a set schedule or time frame.

1.4.2 Who is a project/program manager?

Sometimes referred to as a program manager, a project manager creates an action plan for all the teams to timely carry out a project. To accomplish this, they will define the project's scope and cost, set up an effective communication system for all the teams involved in the project, and monitor each stage of the project execution. Project managers ensure that the projects they are managing are completed within a set schedule and with the right features.

To encourage maximum participation in the project, a project manager may lead meetings, consistently discuss with the teams and stakeholders, work on project budgeting and resource planning, and guide teams in adherence to the initial project plan. In short, it is the project manager who keeps everyone's focus on the project so that it can be completed on time.

The main difference between a project manager, a scrum manager, and a product manager is that a product manager oversees the ideation, design, and strategy of a product whereas a project manager manages the actual development and production (engineering) of the product-making, while a scrum master ensures adherence to the scrum principles for agile development.

Chapter Summary

- Organizations need product managers to help them champion their new products or refine the existing ones. As a result, product managers are tasked to oversee the entire lifecycle of a product, from its ideation to its design, development, production, launch, and distribution.
- A day in a product manager's life sees them participate in meetings with all stakeholders that are associated with the product, connect and communicate with them, undertake research, and engage in strategic product planning.
- A project manager oversees all the processes leading to the creation of a new product or refinement of an existing one. On the other hand, a product manager handles a product's complete Product Lifecycle Management (PLM).
- A scrum master ensures that a project team adheres to implementing scrum principles while working on a project. A scrum master brings both the product owners (managers) and project managers together to seamlessly work on the project.

Quiz

1. Which of the following isn't a product manager's goal?
   a. To hold team members to the best scrum principles
   b. To plan, design, and develop product
   c. To undertake concurrent product research

2. Another word for "project manager" is ...
   a. product manager
   b. program manager
   c. Scrum master

3. The process of making a miniature version of a product before mass-producing it is referred to as....
   a. product lifecycle
   b. prototyping
   c. launch

4. What differentiates a project manager from a product manager is that the former focuses primarily on....
   a. product development
   b. executing projects
   c. scrum arrangement

5. Which of the expressions below is NOT correct?
   a. Project managers are product owners.
   b. Product managers can use customers' feedback to refine a product.
   c. Scrum masters are not project managers but project facilitators.

6. ... are not part of the Scrum team.
   a. Project managers
   b. Customers
   c. Product managers

7. Which of these processes isn't a product manager's core responsibility?
   a. Product conceptualization
   b. Product development
   c. Product lifecycle management

8. One of the benefits of having a winning product for organizations is to....
   a. increase or maintain its revenue
   b. hire a few product managers
   c. lose money

9. ... are professionals tasked with managing teams working on a project so as to ensure the project is completed on time and within schedule.
   a. Product managers
   b. Project managers
   c. Scrum masters

10. A typical example of an intangible product is....
    a. a cell phone
    b. cloud technology service
    c. a vehicle

Answers

1 – a	2 – b	3 – b	4 – b	5 – a
6 – b	7 – b	8 – a	9 – b	10 – b

Self-Learning Management Series

Chapter 2
Identifying Product Opportunities

Key Learning Objectives
- Understanding customer needs and market analysis
- Opportunity hypothesis and competition in a market
- Segmentation, Targeting, and Positioning (STP)
- Converting product vision into strategy
- Understanding user and buyer personas, business model canvas, user group, research, and customer interactions

It is not practical or sensible for companies to build new products and then start looking for consumers to sell them to. Many organizations have lost large amounts of their financial resources for failing to conduct thorough market research before building their products.

Consumers make buying decisions based on their urgent needs—in other words, no one wants to buy a product simply because it is beautifully made—people usually buy a product that will help them solve a particular problem they are grappling with. Knowing their customers' problems beforehand can present some amazing product opportunities for organizations.

2.1 Market Analysis and Understanding Customers' Needs

Market analysis involves conducting market-related inquiries through industry analysts' reports, surveys, and customer conversations to better understand customer preferences.[4] Once the customer preferences and opportunities are well understood, the organization can consider bringing the product/solution to the market to satisfy customer needs. Market analysis generates new insights and causes the organization's management to look inwardly for solutions to some of the market-based challenges that an organization can solve for the customers.

2.2 Opportunity Hypothesis

If an organization has successfully identified certain "important needs" to be met in the market, technically referred to as the "product opportunity", the organization still needs to engage in opportunity hypothesis testing to ensure that the product idea is viable.

Opportunity hypothesis, in product management, can be described as the process of validating the significance of a product idea to make sure it is sensible enough and can do what it is expected to do. Consequently, the hypothesis will ensure that an organization is able to generate sufficient revenue from the product. Companies are in business to

---

[4]. Faridani, A. (2021). Why Businesses Can't Afford to Skip Market Research. Forbes, retrieved from https://www.forbes.com

make some revenue from their products/services. Otherwise, there is no point in setting up such companies.

A hypothesis is a tentative assumption made in order to draw out and test its logical or empirical consequences.[5] Companies need to find plausible answers to the following hypothesis questions:

- *Who are our target users/consumers/demographics/customer segments?*
- *What problem is our product trying to solve in their lives?*
- *What significant impact do we expect the product to have?*
- *How much impact do we have and for how long can we sustain it?*

The answers to the questions above can be used in formulating an effective opportunity hypothesis. It is imperative to utilize feedback from stakeholders, including customers, prospective users, and industry experts to validate the opportunity hypothesis.

Product managers (PMs) often come up with a set of questions that will allow them to understand customer preferences and the potential impact of the new product that they are considering building. It is really important to understand the customers' willingness to pay for the product in order to ensure that the product will be able to generate sufficient revenue to justify the investment.

Even after the initial opportunity is validated, it is necessary to continuously refine the opportunity based on additional inputs received from the market as well as from the customers.

---

5. Hypothesis. 2024. In *Merriam-Webster.com* Retrieved February 5, 2024, from https://www.merriam-webster.com

2.3 Competition

More often than not, multiple companies may be working on creating a similar product, possibly targeting the same customer segments or markets. Undoubtedly, this will cause serious competition among the companies as they compete for the same customer demographic. Failing to be well-prepared to outperform its competitors can hurt an organization in many ways, such as experiencing a sharp reduction in market share, losing tangible percent of its annual revenue, and struggling with cash flow that may threaten the survival of the organization.

Once the competition is understood, it is important to identify the key differentiation for the product that PMs are considering building. Essentially, it explains how the product will be different from other similar products in the market and why customers would consider buying it.

A typical example of how product competition works can be seen in the rivalry between two giant smartphone makers, Apple, Inc., and Samsung. Despite the fact that both Samsung and Apple, Inc. are smartphone manufacturers, Apple, Inc. is perceived as a high-quality leader in the industry because of Apple's brand and ease of use. On the other hand, Samsung is known for providing low-cost smartphones and a wide variety of free apps.

2.4 Segmentation, Targeting, and Positioning (STP)

To outperform their competitors, organizations adopt the Segmentation, Targeting, and Positioning (STP) approach. This involves identifying which customer segment to concentrate on and then building the product/services for that customer segment.

This process can be divided into three parts:

2.4.1 Segmentation

This involves categorizing customers based on their preferential interests in an organization's product(s). They could be existing or future customers, who have displayed an intention in purchasing the organization's products. Consumers can be divided into different market segments in accordance with their financial status, demographics, educational level, geographical region, etc. The following are the typical variables or denominators for consumer segmentation:

- **Demographics:** Gender, age, education, income, etc.
- **Behavior:** Loyalty, benefit, readiness stage, status, usage, etc.
- **Psychographic:** Traits, attitudes, wants, expertise, needs, etc.
- **Geography:** Country, city, rural, region, etc.

2.4.2 Targeting

Once the consumers are divided into segments, targeting allows the organization to identify one or more consumer segments for which it would be worth building the product. While identifying one or more target segments for the product, product managers need to consider if the segments are:

1. **Measurable:** Organizations need to identify the number of customers in each segment, understand their buying patterns, and estimate the revenue opportunities from each segment.

2. **Substantial:** Organizations should focus on the substantial customer segment because it will pay off in the end. A substantial segmentation has an adequate number of customers who are interested in buying the organization's product/solution. Whatever amount the organization has spent on building and marketing the product to the target customer segment will be worth an effort in the long run.
3. **Accessible:** The customer segment must be reachable via communication and distribution efforts.
4. **Actionable:** The organization should be able to offer a valuable product/solution that each targeted customer segment wants.

2.4.3 Positioning

Consumers need to be informed upfront about what benefits they can derive from using a product. This is what is referred to as product positioning. Customers, on their part, are so consistently inundated with advertisements and sales messages that they will only respond to what tickles their fancy. That is why even really good products can fail in the market if they are not positioned correctly to the customers. **Geoffrey Moore has recommended the following format for the value proposition statement: For (target customers) who (statement of the need or opportunity), the (product name) is a (product category) that (statement of the key benefit—that is, compelling reason to buy). Unlike (primary competitive alternative), our product (statement of primary differentiation).**[6]

---

6. GRIN tech. "Geoffrey Moore Positioning Statement with Examples," April 8, 2019. https://the.gt/geoffrey-moore-positioning-statement/.

Here are a couple of examples of product positioning statements:

- **For EcoClean:** *For environmentally-conscious homeowners, EcoClean is an all-natural cleaning solution that safely removes tough stains and odors. As a useful alternative to cleaners with chemicals, EcoClean is made with plant-based ingredients and ensures a healthy home environment.*

- **For a Lifestyle app:** *For busy professionals who aspire to enhance their work-life balance, LifeHelper is a handy lifestyle app that provides personalized wellness tips, habit tracking, and goal setting. Unlike other productivity tools, LifeHelper can be smoothly integrated into your day-to-day routine, offering real-time insights and helpful recommendations.*

Some interesting facts about consumers' preferences[7]

- It is believed that 71% of consumers admire brands that provide personalized shopping experience (2019).

- It was discovered that brands can significantly extend their reach to consumers if they adopt omnichannel strategies such as using emails (37%), text messages (17%), social media advertising (14%), phone calls (14%), social media (20%), TV advertising (37%), podcasting content (4%), and digital advertising (16%) (2020).

- A third of consumers will be willing to pay premium prices for products they believe are sustainable (2021).

---

7. "Consumer Behavior Statistics You Should Know in 2024 [New Data]." Accessed November 29, 2024. https://blog.hubspot.com

2.5 Vision → Strategy

All the products that are introduced in the market go through the steps shown in Figure 2.1. In this section, we will look at how a product vision is converted into a product strategy. Converting a strategy to a roadmap will be discussed in Chapter Three.

Figure 2.1 The product development process

Source: Adapted from ProductPlan. "The Ultimate Guide to Product Strategy." Accessed November 29, 2024. https://www.productplan.com

2.5.1 What is a product vision?

Every company has a unique vision which is, in essence, a "motivational statement" that details what the products are designed to achieve. It describes the goals and usefulness of the final products. Organizations use their "product visions" to describe the long-term mission and purpose of the product.

Some popular examples of product visions are highlighted below[8]:

- **Zoom:** *"To make video communication frictionless."*
- **LinkedIn:** *"To create economic opportunity for every member of the global workforce."*
- **Instagram:** *"To capture and share the world's moments."*

---

8. Fard, Adam. "10 Best Product Vision Statement Examples That Actually Work (And Why)." Adamfard. December 6, 2024. https://adamfard.com/blog/10-best-product-vision-statement-examples

- **Google:** *"To provide access to the world's information in one click."*
- **Netflix:** *"To become the world's leading streaming entertainment service."*
- **Uber:** *"Evolving the way the world moves."*

The above-stated "inspirational statements" are then built into products to reflect the companies' global goals and ambitions.

2.5.2 What is product strategy?

The next step after defining the product vision is building the product strategy. A product strategy essentially guides the company toward achieving the product vision. As shown in Figure 2.2, a great product strategy includes three important elements.

Figure 2.2 Elements of product strategy

Source: Pichler, Roman. "Elements of an Effective Product Strategy." *Roman Pichler* (blog), May 19, 2015. https://www.romanpichler.com.

1. **Market and needs:** Organizations need to investigate whether the market is ripe for their products and whether consumers are desirous of having those products. It is practically counterproductive and wasteful for a company to spend its resources to build a product that no one wants to purchase. An organization could draw an important conclusion from its initial market research and analysis about whether consumers will be interested in its new product.
2. **Business goals:** For-profit organizations are in business to fulfill their business goals. So, it is important that the strategy of the organization aligns with the corporate objectives and it will allow the company to achieve the business goals.
3. **Key features & differentiators:** The product strategy should reflect the amazing features and capabilities that differentiate a company's product from that of its competitors. Differentiation of the product should be valuable, rare, and shouldn't be easy to replicate for the competitors. For example, Apple, Inc.'s iPhones are very popular globally because a large number of smartphone users find the iPhone's features to be quite useful, exciting, and easy to use.

The following are the components of a good product strategy:

1. A well-defined product vision
2. The target audience of the product.
3. The product's unique selling point differentiates it from competitors.
4. The stakeholders involved in the management of the product.[9]

---

9. LeMay, M. (2017). Product Management in Practice: A Real-World Guide to the Key Connective Role of the 21st Century. Sebastopol, CA: O'Reilly Media, 65.

Once the strategy for the product is finalized, PMs need to come up with a product roadmap that can bring the product strategy into reality. The product roadmap will be discussed in detail in Chapter Three.

2.6 User and Buyer Personas

Oftentimes, organizations struggle to fully understand who their target customers are and their needs. When this happens, they may not be effectively building and marketing their products in the right way, thereby limiting product adoption.

To overcome this serious issue, companies need to create a user and buyer persona for each of their products.

- **A user persona** is a fictitious caricature of an ideal user of a product: What demographic do they belong to? Why will they be using the products? What are their pain points? What are their day-to-day activities and what are their daily goals?
- **A buyer persona** is a fictitious representation of what an ideal buyer may look like: Why will they be paying for the products? What is their economic or social status? What are their shopping preferences and trends? How do they like to be served? What can motivate them to buy more of the product?

It should be stated that a user persona is technically different from a buyer persona, even though they are often used interchangeably. A user might not always be the buyer of a product. A simple example of this would be parents buying toys for their kids. Parents pay for the toys while the kids play with those toys. In this case, parents are the buyers while kids are the users.

It is very important for an organization to successfully draw up a correct user and buyer persona from the bulk of data/information it has already obtained through the preceding market research and analysis.

2.7 Business Model Canvas

A business model canvas provides a visual representation of key aspects of the business. It allows product managers and entrepreneurs to easily analyze and communicate their strategy with various stakeholders. The business model canvas allows businesses to understand how different elements of the business or product interact with each other as well as identify potential weaknesses and areas of improvement.

While traditional business plans can be comprehensive and hence cumbersome to read, the business model canvas is a single-page document that allows businesses to visualize the most important aspects of their business. That is why it is heavily used in startups as companies plan to launch a new product and generate revenue for the same. In the startup world, it is also used to communicate companies' visions to partners, investors, and employees. Creating a business model canvas is equally useful even if the company has an existing product that is generating revenue, as it allows the organization to assess its business plan and refine its strategy to reach its goals.

The figure below shows the standard template of the business model canvas. As shown, it consists of nine elements key to the business. These elements, along with the business model canvas, are covered in detail in Chapter 8.

Figure 2.3 — A standard business model canvas template

KEY PARTNERS	KEY ACTIVITIES	VALUE PROPOSITIONS	CUSTOMER RELATIONSHIPS	CUSTOMER SEGMENTS
Who are our key partners? Who are our key suppliers? Which key resources are we acquiring from our partners? Which key activities do partners perform?	What key activities do our value propositions require? Our distribution channels? Customer relationships? Revenue streams?	What value do we deliver to the customer? Which one of our customers' problems are we helping to solve? What bundles of products and services are we offering to each segment? Which customer needs are we satisfying? What is the minimum viable product?	How do we get, keep, and grow customers? Which customer relationships have we established? How are they integrated with the rest of our business model? How costly are they?	For whom are we creating value? Who are our most important customers? What are the customer archetypes?
	KEY RESOURCES What key resources do our value propositions require? Our distribution channels? Customer relationships? Revenue streams?		**CHANNELS** Through which channels do our customer segments want to be reached? How do other companies reach them now? Which ones work best? Which ones are most cost-efficient? How are we integrating them with customer routines?	

COST STRUCTURE	REVENUE STREAMS
What are the most important costs inherent to our business model? Which key resources are most expensive? Which key activities are most expensive?	For what value are our customers really willing to pay? For what do they currently pay? What is the revenue model? What are the pricing tactics?

Source: "Create a New Business Model Canvas - Canvanizer." https://canvanizer.com

2.8 Users' Group and Customer Interactions

An organization requires plenty of data/information about its current and prospective customers to be able to make strategic decisions about its product and capabilities. Some of the avenues a company can employ in gathering useful information about its customers include utilizing user groups, research, and customer interactions.

- **Users' group:** This involves putting some existing and new users of a particular product in a focus group where they are advised to freely give their opinions about the product and areas of improvement and provide visibility into initiatives they are taking so the company can build their strategy around it.

- **Customer interactions:** A company can learn so much about its product (both new and existing ones) by regularly interacting with its customers. An organization can interact with its customers via phone/video calls, emails, tech events, and so on. Customer interactions should be consistent to ensure product adoption as well as to gather feedback about the product directly from the customers. These interactions allow a company to discover how its customers perceive its products. Customers are often encouraged with freebies, discounts, and other rewards for actively participating in the company's forums, social media discussions, etc.

Chapter Summary

- Through market research, organizations can discover various product opportunities, which means they can understand consumers' pain points and what they want right now.
- Segmentation, Targeting, and Positioning (STP) help an organization to get its product to the right consumers who are willing and able to purchase it.
- Every company has a rival or competitor, and the only pragmatic approach to doing better in the already crowded market or industry is for that company to engage in continuous and effective market research and analysis and educate customers on how their product is different from that of the competitors.
- A user persona is a fictitious caricature of an ideal user of a product while a buyer persona is a fictitious representation of what an ideal buyer looks like.
- It is important that an organization devises a product strategy that will actualize its product vision.
- A Business Model Canvas provides a visual representation of key aspects of the business and it allows product managers and entrepreneurs to easily analyze and communicate their strategy with various stakeholders.
- Users' groups, research, and customer interactions are necessary for gathering the all-important customers' feedback and data/information.

Quiz

1. A ... is a fictitious caricature of an ideal user of a product.
   a. seller persona
   b. user persona
   c. buyer persona

2. What differentiates a user persona from a buyer persona?
   a. They are the same.
   b. A user persona is only about the representation of the actual user of a product.
   c. A user persona is only about the representation of the buyer of a product.

3. Which of the following is NOT one of the best approaches for soliciting useful information from customers?
   a. Users' group
   b. Customer interactions
   c. Product ideation

4. Why should an organization divide its customers into segments?
   a. To know exactly what each customer segment needs and wants to purchase the product
   b. To be able to give them freebies
   c. To force them to buy a product they don't necessarily need

5. Which of these research methods is NOT used by companies to better know their customers' preferences?
   a. Market research
   b. Market analysis
   c. Supply chain analysis

6. A... is a document prepared by a company that is necessary for it to achieve its product vision.
   a. Product strategy
   b. Product design
   c. Product pricing

7. Technically, an organization's product vision and product strategy mean the same thing.
   a. False
   b. True

8. .... is a motivational statement written by organizations and shows the details of what their products are designed to achieve their goals and their usefulness.
   a. Product strategy
   b. Product marketing
   c. Product vision

9. ..., in product management, can be described as the process of validating the significance of a product opportunity.
   a. Product development
   b. Opportunity hypothesis
   c. Users' group

10. ... is a strategic management template that can be used by any company to design a new business model or improve its existing one while developing a new product line.
    a. Pricing model template
    b. Business model canvas
    c. Customer Relationships Management (CRM) model

Answers

1 – b	2 – b	3 – c	4 – a	5 – c
6 – a	7 – a	8 – a	9 – b	10 – b

Chapter 3
Converting Strategy into a Product

Key Learning Objectives

- Building a roadmap from a product strategy
- Feature prioritization models and frameworks
- Crafting product requirements/specifications
- Difference between waterfall and agile methodologies
- Building an MVP/prototype to launch PoC/private preview
- Product pricing and launching the product

As briefly covered in Chapter Two, product strategy is a high-level organization's blueprint for ideation, designing, developing, and then launching an entirely new product or refining an existing one. This chapter will elaborate on how a strategy can be converted into a final product. We will learn the various steps necessary for building a product that aligns with the strategy and vision of the organization. We will also understand the role of the PM in all these processes.

3.1 Strategy → Roadmap

As learned in Chapter Two, a product strategy allows product managers to translate the product vision into a final product. Product strategy acts as a guiding post while creating a roadmap for the product and prioritizing the right features. As indicated in Figure 3.1, drafting an effective product strategy is a prerequisite for creating a realistic product plan and a useful product roadmap.[10]

Figure 3.1 The product development process

Source: Adapted from ProductPlan. "The Ultimate Guide to Product Strategy." Accessed November 29, 2024. https://www.productplan.com

3.1.1 What is a product roadmap?

A product roadmap covers all the required features, along with the milestones and target dates, to make the product vision a reality. It basically puts the product strategy into action by setting realistic milestones. There are multiple ways to create a product roadmap, as described below:

1. **Goal-based product roadmap:** This roadmap is created to fulfill a product goal, usually within a set deadline. This roadmap divides the deadlines based on the goals that need to be achieved within that time frame. Figure 3.2 shows a sample of a goal-based product roadmap.

---

10. Lombardo, C.T., McCarthy, B., Ryan, E., Connors, M. (2017). Product Roadmaps Relaunched: How to Set Direction while Embracing Uncertainty. Sebastopol, CA: O'Reilly Media, 44.

Figure 3.2 Goal-oriented product roadmap

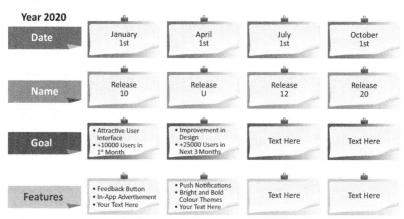

Source: Adapted from Eyo, Iniobong. "What Kind of Product Roadmap Is Right for Your Team? | Appcues Blog." Accessed November 29, 2024. https://www.appcues.com

2. **Featured-based product roadmap:** This kind of roadmap outlines the essential features that should be built into a product. It will also indicate the target dates by which the features have to be built. The example shown in Figure 3.3 shows how the product managers can divide their roadmap into different areas including growing consumers, growing enterprise customers, reducing churn, and so on. Each of these areas would have features that would allow product managers to achieve the product goals and increase product adoption.

Figure 3.3 Feature-based roadmap for consumer growth scalability

	Q3 2017	Q4 2017	Q1 2017	Q2 2017
Milestones	⚑ Beta Launch		⚠ First 100 DAUs ⚠	First 1000 DAUs
Consumer Growth	Auto Save	Auto Sync		Menu Wide Options
	Conversion Tracking	Real Time Mirroring		
		Google Single Sign on		
Enterprise Growth	Multi Language	CRM Integration	SQL Support	
	Co-worker Invitation	Executive View		Stakeholder Commenting
Scalability	Geo-locations	Handle Larger Data Sets		Features Prioritization Tracking
		Offline Support	Issue Map	
Decrease Churn	Advanced Interactions	Sharing		
	New Like Notification		Custom Colours and Backgrounds	
		Performance Improvement		

Source: Adapted from "Feature Roadmap Consumer Growth Scalability Quarterly Timeline," July 22, 2021. https://www.slideteam.ne

In reality, it may be challenging to choose the most appropriate product roadmap, but the best practice is to go for a roadmap that puts factors such as market volatility, product age, and roadmap audience into consideration.

3.2 Feature Prioritization

While a product manager would like to have so many features built for the product, not all of them can be built right away due to team resources and skills, lack of time, and bandwidth to accommodate additional features, current organizational goals, and other challenges.

This calls for feature prioritization, which is the process of determining which features will be built first while others may be delayed to a certain period in the future. Due to some of the constraints already listed above, such as budget and giving preferences to products with a high return on investment (ROI), there could be a growing backlog of features that may be attended to in several releases after the initial version of the product has been released. Product managers need to be customer-centric while prioritizing the features to ensure they get the maximum return on investment for the features that the engineering team is building.

At times, product managers may be required to tender substantial data to support their claim that certain features should be given prominence over others. The following frameworks can be utilized for feature prioritization:

3.2.1 The Kano Model Theory

The Kano Model Theory explains that customers derive maximum satisfaction from products that have all the useful features they want.

Figure 3.4   **The Kano Method Theory**

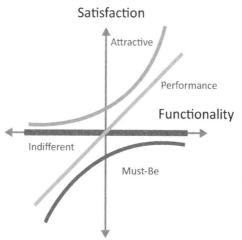

Source: Folding Burritos. "The Complete Guide to the Kano Model," June 5, 2015. https://foldingburritos.com/blog/kano-model/

In Figure 3.4 above, the vertical axis stands for the satisfaction levels of consumers (from dissatisfied at the bottom to highly satisfied at the top) and the horizontal axis stands for the functionality/features of the product (from least useful on the left to most useful on the right). The graph also reveals the four different kinds of features, namely "attractive features", "performance-based" features, "must-be" features, and "indifferent" features. From the graph, it is clearly evident that all features that are essential for the "performance" of the product have a linear relationship with customer satisfaction.

The "must-be" features are those that the consumers expect to be in a product by default. Even if these features are highly functional, they might not add to their satisfaction levels, as they expect those features by default(thus the curve never goes to the positive side of the satisfaction axis). On the other hand, "attractive" features excite the customers and greatly improve satisfaction. Lastly, "indifferent" features are those whose presence or absence doesn't make any difference to satisfaction.

3.2.2 The RICE Model

This model specifically concentrates on four areas that can be used in adjudging the priority of a product feature when compared with others. The four areas to check in a particular feature are based on the RICE acronym.[11]

- **Reach:** How many users or customers are affected by your product? The reach score is the number that is estimated.

---

11. ProductPlan. "RICE Scoring Model." https://www.productplan.com/glossary/rice-scoring-model/.

- **Impact:** How will the feature bring about a better customer experience (usually scored from 0.25-3)? This is the extent to which the feature will contribute to user satisfaction, revenue, and retention. You can score based on the following scale:

  3 = massive impact

  2 = high impact

  1 = medium impact

  0.5 = low impact

  0.25 = minimal impact

- **Confidence:** How confident is the product manager about the importance of this particular feature? (this is awarded a percentage out of 100).

  100% = high confidence

  80% = medium confidence

  50% = low confidence

- **Effort:** How much effort is required to build this feature? (Effort is estimated on a scale of 1-5). The effort is considered as the total amount of work required to complete the project. It is usually measured in person-months or person-hours. For example, if your feature requires 3 months for people to complete it, your score will be 3.

The next thing to do is to estimate the RICE score using this formula: **(Reach × Impact × Confidence)/ Effort.**

Here's an example of how you would score a feature using the RICE framework.

Reach: Let's assume there are 50,000 users of a product's feature. This will be the reach.

Impact: Let's give a rating of 2 to our particular feature in terms of impact.

Confidence: 50% (0.50) This is the PM's confidence in the feature.

Effort: Let's rate the effort required to create a product at a 4.

Hence, using (Reach × Impact × Confidence)/ Effort, the RICE score is:

(50,000 users × 2 × 0.50)/4 = 12,500

To know if the feature's RICE score is high enough, it is advisable to compare it with the RICE scores of other features while deciding the feature priority. The higher the RICE score, the higher the feature priority. It is usually sensible to select a feature with high impact but low effort if the confidence is pretty high. The main drawback of utilizing the RICE score is that confidence and impact scores are hardly 100 percent accurate.

3.2.3 The MoSCoW Method

MoSCoW stands for "must-have," "should-have," "could-have," and "won't-have." Product managers utilize this method to prioritize features they would like to build for their product. They can use the outcome of the MoSCoW method to persuade their organizations' stakeholders to obtain consensus and ensure that those features are eventually built into the product.

- **Must-have:** These are critical, non-negotiable features that will give the product under development its unique usefulness. It is vital to include must-have features in the Minimal Viable Product (MVP), because the absence of these essential features will mostly render the product not useful for the customer (MVP will be discussed later in this chapter.)

- **Should-have:** These are relatively important features but they are not perceived as must-haves. A product can still function properly without should-have features, but with them, the product could have fared better.
- **Could-have:** These are nice features to have in a product but they are good to have features and can be considered for future iterations of the product.
- **Won't-have:** These are usually low-impact and low-priority features; they are normally put at the bottom of the wish list.

With the MoSCoW Method, product managers can influence the direction of product development, ensuring that preference is given to *must-have* features. It is equally advisable that product managers, based on their own personal biases, should not mistake *could-have* or *should-have* features for *must-have* ones. By undertaking some organization-wide consultations, it is possible to achieve a broad consensus or agreement on the level of impact or priority of each feature in the product. Figure 3.5 shows an example of categorizing various features according to the MoSCow method. This example indicates the related requirements when developing an app.

| Figure 3.5 | An example of the MoSCow method |

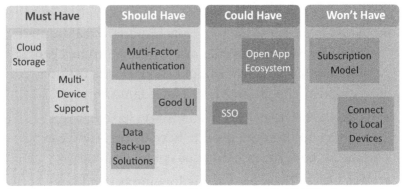

Source: "What Is the MoSCoW Method & How Does It Work? | Vibe." Accessed January 22, 2025. https://vibe.us/blog/moscow-method/

3.2.4 The Buy-a-Feature Game

Customers and stakeholders can select their most desirable "must-have" or "should-have" features for a product by merely playing a game. The game is called buy-a-feature. Product managers utilize the outcomes of this game to get a feeling of the stakeholders' confidence toward certain features that may ultimately increase its RICE framework score. This is how to play the buy-a-feature game:

1. Each player is given a fixed amount of money to spend on purchasing their desirable features. Depending on their preferences, stakeholders and customers can choose feature ideas and give them monetary value. At the end of the game, the product manager can gather input from all the stakeholders to understand the priorities of a wide range of customers and prioritize the features accordingly.

2. Once the game is over, players should be asked to state the reasons for choosing some features over others. Their responses could provide invaluable insights for the product managers overseeing that product lifecycle. They will be able to build new capacities to meet customers' changing demands, thereby improving the overall customer satisfaction for the products.

3.2.5 Opportunity Scoring

Opportunity scoring, which is sometimes known as "gap analysis" or "opportunity analysis", helps product managers identify features that customers consider as underdeveloped but relatively very important.

This technique depends mainly on customers' feedback in accordance with their preferences. Opportunity scoring may be a useful method for product managers to discover additional opportunities in their existing products.

For this approach, customers are surveyed and asked to rank product features on a scale of 1-5 while responding to the two questions below:

- *How important or useful do they think this feature is?*
- *How satisfied are they with the current solution for this feature provided by the product?*

After collecting the scores, the numbers should be plotted on a graph, as shown in Figure 3.6.

| Figure 3.6 | The opportunity scoring |

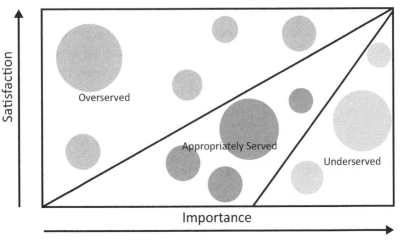

Source: Customer Led Development & Building Better Products. "How to Prioritize Product Features (11 Frameworks with Examples)," December 22, 2021. https://rapidr.io/blog/feature-prioritization/.

Use the following steps to plot an opportunity scoring graph:

1. Gather the data from consumers ranking how important and satisfactory the features of the product are. Here's an example of the data you might receive.

Feature	Satisfaction (S)	Importance (I)
Feature A	3	5
Feature B	2	4
Feature C	4	3
Feature D	1	5
Feature E	3	2

2. Calculate their opportunity score using the following formula:

   Opportunity Score = (Importance−Satisfaction) × Importance

3. Present the opportunity scores for each feature as shown below:

Feature	Satisfaction (S)	Importance (I)	Opportunity Score (I − S) * I
A	3	5	(5 − 3) * 5 = 10
B	2	4	(4 − 2) * 4 = 8
C	4	3	(3 − 4) * 3 = −3
D	1	5	(5 − 1) * 5 = 20
E	3	2	(2 − 3) * 2 = −2

4. Then plot the data on a scatter graph, using the total opportunity score against each feature's score. You can then identify which feature falls under the "overserved," "Appropriately served," or "underserved" section of the graph.

It is important to note that, the higher the opportunity score, the more urgent it is to improve the feature. Product managers can conclude from the scoring what features customers want to be improved and why they aren't satisfied with the current solution provided by the product. The major drawback of this method is that customers may overestimate or underestimate the impact of a feature. This is why it is advisable to select a few informed customers to participate in the scoring to obtain reliable outcomes.

What feature prioritization strategy should a product manager adopt?

Well, there is no fixed answer to this question, because organizations employ whichever prioritization technique they are conversant with and have been quite successful for them.

3.3 Crafting Product Specifications/ Requirements

Once the right feature is prioritized by the product manager, the next step is to write detailed product requirements so that the engineering, UX, and IT teams can start working on building the feature and UX mockups with the right functionality and specifications. The document that lists all the product requirements is known as a Product Requirements Document (PRD).

There are two intrinsic reasons why it is important to have the detailed product requirements for the features:

- **Product consistency:** Product specification helps product managers and other stakeholders ascertain that the product is built with the right features and specifications to satisfy the customers for whom the product is built.
- **Streamlined collaboration:** When the product requirements are specified and known to all teams working on the product, from design and engineering to marketing, they will be able to productively collaborate on choices and tradeoffs throughout the development process. It also allows the product managers and engineering team to ensure the end product delivered to the customers

meets all the requirements specified in the PRD (Product Requirements Document).[12]

It is imperative to fully understand the business case for a product before deciding to write a Product Requirements Document (PRD) for it. To craft effective product specifications/requirements, the following areas related to the product must be clearly highlighted:

- **Product/feature summary:** A product summary is a succinct and vivid account of everything related to the product or feature, highlighting the product's unique proposition, quality features, and how it fulfills the organization's goals and vision.[13]
- **User and buyer personas:** It is equally important to describe the buyer and user personas for the product. This could be a segment of an organization's customer base. This step is helpful in building products that will satisfy target customers' needs.
- **Business case:** This involves describing the expected impact of the product on customer acquisition, revenue, profit, and cost of building the product as well as potential risks.

Once the business case is approved and the product is funded, the next step is to write the detailed Product Requirements Document (PRD).

---

12. Lombardo, C.T., McCarthy, B., Ryan, E., Connors, M. (2017). Product Roadmaps Relaunched: How to Set Direction while Embracing Uncertainty. Sebastopol, CA: O'Reilly Media, 44.

13. Sandy, K. (2020). The Influential Product Manager. Oakland, California: Berrett-Koehler Publishers.

3.3.1 Key elements of a product requirements document (PRD)

Here are the key elements of the PRD:

- **Product descriptions:** The product's intended use, functionality, and purpose must be clearly described.

- **Problem statement** - What problem are we trying to solve for the customer?

- **Customer interest** - Which customers are interested in this, along with the potential monetary value associated with the opportunity?

- **Acceptance criteria:** Acceptance criteria are the features/functionality that must be satisfied to ensure end customers can use the product as intended by the product manager. Acceptance criteria should cover usability, interoperability, performance, and scaling requirements among other things.

  - **Usability requirements:** How will the customer obtain and use the product? Is it by going to the company website or do they need to install the product? Will the customers use UI, Command Line, and/or APIs to use the product?

  - **Interoperability:** It is important to think about how well the product will work with other products offered by the organization. What platforms will be supported? What will be the application programming interface (API) requirements?

  - **Performance and scale requirements:** What are the performance expectations for the product with various features turned ON? How much and how fast is software expected to scale in the case of increased performance requirements from the customer side?

- In the case of hardware products, the PRD would also have information about physical attributes such as weight, operating temperature, and power supply.
- **Milestones and timelines:** The PRD should cover various milestones and expected timelines for each milestone of the product so that the engineering team can plan the design and resources accordingly.

Note that the sections covered in the PRD will vary based on the type of the product, whether the product/feature is a brand new product or an improvement of the existing product.[14]

3.3.2 Creating user stories, function specifications, and test plan

Once the PRD is reviewed and approved by all the stakeholders, the next step is to create User Stories, Functional Specifications (FS), and a test plan to guide the development of the product.

- **User stories:** The product manager or product owner will break down the requirements into user stories so that it is easy for the engineering team to consume the requirements and estimate the effort/resources needed to build the product. User stories also have detailed acceptance criteria, consistent with the acceptance criteria covered in the PRD.
- **Functional specifications (specs):** A functional specification document, often referred to as Functional spec (FS) is the document created by the development team to plan the architecture and design of the product. FS should ensure all the acceptance criteria specified in the PRD

---

14. LeMay, M. (2022) Product Management in Practice: A Practical, Tactical Guide for Your First Day and Every Day After. Sebastopol, California: O' Reilly Media.

are met to ensure the product will be useful for the end customers.

- **Test plan:** The test plan is the document created by the Quality Assurance (QA) team to document the test scenarios/cases that will be tested to ensure the product quality before it is delivered to the customers. The QA team needs to thoroughly understand how the customers will use the product so that they can test the product and ensure product quality.

3.4 Building the Product - Waterfall vs Agile

Once the PRD is reviewed, and user stories, FS, and test plans are created, the engineering team will start building the product. The engineering team can follow different methodologies such as Waterfall and Agile to build the product in a timely manner.

3.4.1 Waterfall

Waterfall, so to speak, is a regimented way of managing a product life cycle. It involves executing well-defined, somehow rigid steps that require that one step is absolutely completed before moving on to the next one. Each step in the process is dated or scheduled and, being a linear approach, a waterfall environment doesn't allow experimenting with multiple options that are not initially parts of the plan. Once a waterfall procedure starts, it progresses toward the last outcome as shown in Figure 3.7.

Figure 3.7 The differences between the waterfall and agile methodologies

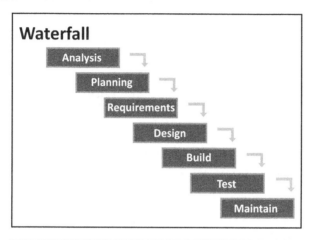

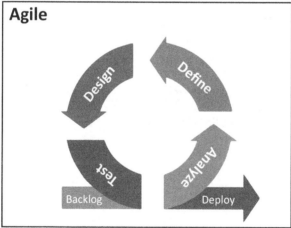

Source: Adapted from RevGen. "When Does Waterfall Project Management Make Sense?" Accessed January 22, 2025. https://www.revgenpartners.com

3.4.2 Agile

In contrast, agile methodology allows process iteration, and flexibility. Unlike the waterfall technique, agile handles the development process in sprints (short, time-based activities), usually one to four weeks in duration. When the needs arise, agile product management teams can quickly change a product's features priority based on customers' feedback and deliver a newer version of the product as soon as possible.

3.4.3 Which is better, agile or waterfall?

Table 3.1 lists the key differences between waterfall and agile. In principle, there are no hard and fast rules for selecting either waterfall or agile methodology. However, it is generally believed that the agile methodology works better for building software products that can be modified easily while the waterfall methodology works better for building hardware products.

Table 3.1 Waterfall vs. agile

	Waterfall	Agile
Flexibility	Not flexible, product development must be executed based on the pre-planned steps and schedules	Very flexible, changes can be implemented into a product late in its lifecycle
Stability	Stable because the stages in the process are pre-defined.	Susceptible to fluctuation based on the newly discovered requirements
Customer involvement	Restricts customers' involvement only to the initial feedback	Permits continuous customers' and stakeholders' involvement
Project phases	The phases are systemic, linear, and non-overlapping	Iterative with overlapping phases

	Waterfall	Agile
Testing	Occurs once the product is developed	Can be done concurrently along the product development
Risk management	Issues can only be detected after the product has been developed so more risky	Issues can be detected all along the product development because testing is done for each phase so less risky.

3.5 Building an MVP → Launching the POC/Private Preview

As explained in the previous section, when the agile methodology is used to build the product, getting customer feedback early on in the development cycle is crucial to ensure customer feedback is incorporated and the right end product is built for the customer.

3.5.1 Minimum Viable Product (MVP)

The minimum viable product (MVP) has only the core functionality of the product and it allows product managers to test an idea by providing an early version of the product to the limited target customers and collecting feedback. MVP can be viewed as a risk reduction tool as it reduces the risk of building a product that is not useful for the end customers.

Organizations often have a private preview program, also called an Early Access Program (EAP) to showcase the MVP to the target customers and gather feedback so that the right product can be built for the customers.

3.5.2 Minimum Marketable Feature (MMF) - Also called Minimum Marketable Product (MMP)

The Minimum Marketable Feature (MMF), often called Minimum Marketable Product (MMP), is the product with the smallest feature set that addresses user needs, creates a desire to buy the product, and hence, can be marketed and sold to the customers. It allows the company to reduce time-to-market rather than waiting for the fully featured product to be ready.

Organizations can develop one or more MVPs to test their ideas to gather relevant feedback. Figure 3.8 illustrates this process. MVP versions can range from 1 to any number "n". The feedback gathered from these MVPs can be used to create and launch MMP - a product with the right features that are useful for the customers and hence, can be marketed and sold to the customers.

Figure 3.8 The MVP to MMP process

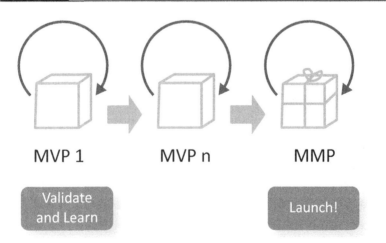

When the product becomes available for the customers to buy, it is often referred to as the General Availability (GA) of the product.

3.6 Product Pricing

Customers buy the product to make their life easy. One of the most important factors in purchase decisions is the price of the product. Therefore, organizations need to consider different pricing methods or models to arrive at the most sensible prices for their products. Here are four unique pricing methods usually employed by the businesses:

- **Value-based pricing:** Using this method, products are priced based on the intrinsic values or benefits that consumers see in them. This happens to be one of the most common pricing approaches, but thorough market research is necessary to decide exactly what kind of value consumers have identified in the products.

- **Competitor-based pricing:** Companies can also base their products' prices on what their competitors are charging for the same products. For example, Company A may be selling a toothbrush for $2 per piece. When company B makes its own toothbrush with similar capabilities, it may decide to price it at exactly $2 or a little below it, say for $1.99, so as to draw more consumers to its product.

- **Cost-plus pricing:** It is not rare for organizations to price their products by taking into account their production cost and the expected profit margin. However, a company may overprice its product if it doesn't conduct the appropriate market research to discover how much its customers are willing to pay for the product. When consumers discover that a product's price doesn't match the benefits that could be derived from it, such a product may not be widely adopted by consumers.

- **Dynamic pricing:** The idea behind dynamic pricing is that a single product can have different prices based on the market segments it is sold to. For example, Microsoft offers a different price for students for all its products, while professionals are expected to pay more for the same products.

3.7 Launching the Product

While this chapter explains how the product is brought to the market from ideation to GA (the General Availability Product), it takes more than just an engineering and product management effort to make the product successful.

It is important that the customers fully understand the benefits of the product and how it is different from the competing products in the market. Salespeople within the company have to be trained so that they can effectively communicate the value of the product to the customers. Additionally, companies have to reinforce the market/customers with consistent messaging across all the channels to create brand awareness of the product in the long run. To achieve that, we need to have a successful Go-To-Market motion (GTM) that will be covered in great detail in the next chapter.

Chapter Summary

- Product vision must be converted into a strategy that will guide the entire product lifecycle management.
- It is imperative to prioritize the number and quality of the features a product can have in its first version. Other features may be added later in the product life cycle.
- Every product has some requirements it must meet, without which consumers may reject it.
- There are two structurally different approaches/methodologies for building the product—waterfall and agile methodologies, and each method has its merits and demerits.
- The MVP will allow organizations to test the idea with the customers before building/launching a full-featured product.
- Minimum Marketable Product (MMP) is the product with the smallest feature set that addresses user needs, creates a desire to buy the product, and hence, can be marketed and sold to the customers.
- Products can be priced through four approaches—value-based, cost-based, competitor-based, and dynamic pricing.

Quiz

1. Product managers use a product strategy to....
   a. Apply for loans
   b. Guide their teams to build the right product for end customers
   c. Hire new recruits

2. The topmost part of a product strategy pyramid is a.....
   a. product roadmap
   b. product plan
   c. product vision

3. Which of the following documents is NOT required for drafting a product roadmap?
   a. Product pricing
   b. Product plans
   c. Product strategy

4. The type of product roadmap specifically created to fulfill a product goal within a set timeframe is called......
   a. Feature-based roadmap
   b. Audience-based roadmap
   c. Goal-based roadmap

5. The process of determining which features should be implemented in the first and succeeding versions of a product is referred to as......
   a. product prioritization
   b. feature prioritization
   c. pricing prioritization

6. The Kano Method states that consumers derive ... from a product that has the functionality that they want.
   a. boredom
   b. satisfaction
   c. sadness

7. The elements of the RICE Method include the following except....
   a. reach
   b. impact
   c. product vision

8. What is the name given to a game that customers and stakeholders can play to purchase any feature that they desire to have in their products?
   a. Kano Method
   b. Buy-A-Feature
   c. RICE Method.

9. The "W" in MoSCoW Method stands for....
   a. must-have
   b. won't-have
   c. should-have

10. **Another name for product** *opportunity scoring* **is.....**
   a. gap analysis
   b. market analysis
   c. buy-a-feature

Answers

1 – b	2 – c	3 – a	4 – c	5 – b
6 – b	7 – c	8 – b	9 – b	10 – a

Chapter 4
Product Messaging and Launching the Product

Key Learning Objectives
- Developing a Go-To-Market (GTM) strategy
- The product buying cycle and messaging
- Launch plan and collateral building
- Announcement, PR, digital, and social media marketing
- Measuring GTM success and post-launch activities

An organization needs to effectively communicate its product's value proposition to those who will buy and use it. Interestingly enough, product launch gives companies the unique opportunity to proactively market their newly created or modified products to consumers/customers. In this chapter, we will learn product messaging and how to create a Go-To-Market (GTM) strategy ahead of the product's launch. We will also discuss measuring success and post-launch activities.

4.1 Developing a Go-To-Market (GTM) Strategy

While creating an amazing product is essential, it is equally important for organizations to create a well-crafted Go-To-Market (GTM) strategy to ensure the product's success. A GTM strategy is essentially an extensive plan to launch and market the product. This plan is necessary for the organization to create awareness about the product's capabilities and its differentiation so that prospective customers would be interested in using the company's product to solve their pain points/problems. A typical GTM strategy comprises of target market profiles, a marketing plan, and a distribution strategy. The coming sections describe all these components in detail.

4.1.1 Target market profiles

A target market profile is an elaborate description of an organization's ideal customers (both user and buyer), including their behaviors, demographics, and psychographics. A PM can utilize the following hypothetical questions to analyze and fully understand a product's target market profile:

1. **Who are the potential customers?** — The initial market and demographic analyses conducted by the organization will provide a list of ideal customers who will find the product useful. It is important to note that the organization needs to understand both buyers and users of the product.

2. **What are their needs?** — These include the ideal customers' problems or pain points that they want to solve with the product.

3. **What are their goals and day-to-day activities?** — This includes their broad goals and what success looks like

for buyers and users. What are they doing to resolve the pain points they are currently facing?

4. **What are their buying behaviors?** —Organizations need to understand their customers' buying patterns or behaviors. Consumer buying behaviors are largely influenced by a number of factors such as their cultural, social, financial, and personal preferences. Organizations need this information to properly segment their customers and target them with the products they will find most useful or helpful.

4.1.2 Marketing Plan

The concept of "product-market fit" describes a situation whereby an organization successfully meets its target markets' or consumers' needs and preferences. It indicates that the product developed by the organization is well-received in the market, and it is truly solving customers' pain points. This will make such a product to be in high demand. However, for a product-market fit to be achieved, the organization must fully understand its customers' needs and desires, as discussed in the previous section.

Highlighting the product's unique value proposition will set it apart from others in the market and result in broad acceptance of the new product. This is known as product messaging. Once the product messaging is created, it is important to use this messaging consistently across all the marketing campaigns, social media, emails, and other marketing channels to create awareness and excitement about the product.

The product marketing team works closely with the product management team to build the right messaging and value proposition for the product to highlight the product's unique features, advantages, and applications to the customers. The product marketing team creates assets such as customer-facing presentations, data sheets, solution notes, blogs, competitive decks, conversation guides, and others and ensures consistent product messaging for all the assets.

The marketing team is responsible for marketing the assets built by the product marketing team through various channels. In the case of selling complex B2B products, product management and GTM teams train salespeople and other technical solution teams so that they can effectively pitch the product to the end customers and this will ultimately allow the organization to acquire customers and generate revenue for the product.

4.1.3 Distribution strategy

An all-important question most companies have is, *"How will our target customers discover and access our products?"*. It is imperative for organizations to come up with a distribution strategy that ensures the product is available to the end customer in the preferred place. Since product managers are well aware of where the target customers would prefer to buy the product, product managers need to collaborate with other teams to ensure the right distribution strategy for the product.

Traditionally, retail stores were heavily used by consumers to get the products they wanted. In the internet era, consumers started using online channels such as Amazon, company websites, and the Facebook marketplace. Now, app stores are also being used by consumers to procure the products.[15]

In the case of B2B products, apart from directly selling the product to the end consumers, additional channels

---

15. Sekaran S. *Product Marketing, Simplified: A Customer-Centric Approach to Take a Product to Market.* (Seattle: Amazon, 2020), 32-44.

such as resellers, channel partners, value-added service providers, and digital marketplaces are commonly used by organizations.

For both B2B and B2C products, organizations need to analyze the cost-effectiveness, reach, and brand alignment of each channel to select the most appropriate one or multiple channels for the effective distribution of their products. The best practice is to pick the channels that align with consumers' preferences, in terms of convenience, speed, and safety.

4.2 Product Positioning

It takes more than simply a fantastic product to stand out in the competitive and already crowded market. A product, newly created or modified, must also be strategically positioned to attract customers' attention. For any organization to establish its brand in the eyes of its target audience, it must have a clear and coherent grasp of its product positioning. A product's "positioning" is all about outlining the target market, the product's key selling point, which is otherwise known as its unique value propositions, and describing how the product is different from rivals' offerings.

Therefore positioning messaging demands certain preparedness; it shouldn't be shoddily crafted, but it must be clear, concise, and impactful. While drafting their positioning, organizations need to:

1. **Know their stories:** Organizations should think of their product as the hero of a story in a popular film. Positioning messaging is about crafting a tale that will meaningfully capture the attention of a target audience. What are the features that make the product different and effective? Imagine telling a group of acquaintances about a product in a way that makes all

of them say, *"Wow, we need that!"*. That is the beauty of knowing one's product story inside and out. Product messaging is about showcasing what makes a product extraordinary, giving that product its own personality, in a true and authentic manner.

2. **Be memorable:** Just like a catchy and melodious song or a funny joke, a product's message needs to stick in people's minds. Positioning messaging is about creating a message that leaves a lasting impression on both new and old customers. McDonald's comes up with *"I'm Lovin' It!"*, which often rings a bell in the customer's minds and they keep loving that brand!

3. **Speak the customer's language:** Positioning messaging is about using words and phrases that resonate well with the target audience. A positioning messaging should be relevant and contain up-to-date information, to show the audience that the organization really knows its audience pretty well and cares about their needs.

It should be noted that product positioning is much broader when compared to product messaging, even though people sometimes use the two terms interchangeably.

In practice, strong positioning and messaging can help a company to:

- **Attract the right customers:** Attracting customers who are a good fit for a brand or product is achievable if the product messaging clearly satisfies the yearning of the target audience.
- **Differentiate its product from competitors:** It will set the company apart in the market, making it easier to win customers.

- **Boost brand awareness:** Effective product messaging resonates with the target demographics, leading to better recall and recognition of the product's unique usefulness.
- **Drive sales and conversions:** A company can be confident of good sales and a good conversion rate when its product messaging is done well.

4.3 Understanding Product Buying Cycle/ Purchase Funnel

The product buying cycle, also known as the marketing or sales cycle, is a patterned process customers go through when contemplating a purchase. It is helpful that every organization understands the pattern buyers (or their targeted customers) go through for effective marketing and promotion strategy. Figure 4.1 depicts the purchase funnel based on the AIDA acronym.

Figure 4.1 The purchase funnel (AIDA)

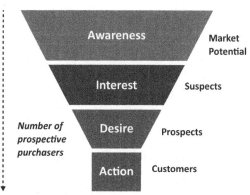

Source: News Powered by Cision. "What Is the AIDA Funnel and How to Optimize It for Your Marketing Strategy?," August 31, 2021. https://news.cision.com

1. **Awareness stage:** The awareness stage is the first step where a consumer becomes conscious of their needs or the desire for a particular product or service. This desire can be influenced by various factors such as personal experiences, recommendations by a friend, or advertisements. For example, a billboard depicting restaurants is often used to trigger hunger in the passersby. This would be the awareness stage for the consumer, after which they will begin exploring the market and gathering information about available options.

2. **Consideration/interest stage:** Once a consumer is aware of his need, he enters the consideration stage by formulating a consideration set and evaluating each option on factors important to him. He/she evaluates different products or services that can fulfill his needs by comparing features, prices, and reviews from previous buyers, to determine the option that best suits his or her requirements. This stage involves extensive research, reading customer reviews, and seeking recommendations from trusted sources. It is also necessary for customers to try out the product and see whether it fits their environment. An organization's ability to convey the benefits of its products that coincide with the target customer needs and differentiation from the competition is crucial during this stage.

3. **Decision stage:** After careful consideration, customers would have narrowed down their options and are ready to make a final decision to purchase. Factors such as ease of use, price, quality, brand reputation, warranties, return policies, after-sales support, and customer service play a crucial role in the decision-making process. Consumers may also consider

additional factors such as their personal preferences, economic conditions, cultural influences, and marketing campaigns' incentives, like discounts, and cash-back guarantees.

4. **Purchase/action stage:** This is the point where a buyer finally determines which product or service best matches his needs and makes a purchase, which can be done online or in physical stores, depending on personal preferences. He may also consider factors such as delivery options, convenience, and availability. It is important to ensure a hassle-free purchasing experience to build customer satisfaction and good recommendations to prospective customers. It is important to capture their contact information in order to develop an ongoing relationship with consumers for future sales.

5. **Post-purchase stage:** While the buying cycle ends with the purchase of the product, gathering customer feedback, reviews and recommendations is equally important as it determines customer satisfaction and future brand loyalty. Positive customer satisfaction can lead to repeat purchases and unconscious word-of-mouth recommendations to others. Likewise, negative experiences can result in customer dissatisfaction and negative reviews. In the case of negative feedback, it is important for the company to take corrective action as soon as possible to ensure customer satisfaction and growth of a company.

4.4 Launch Plan

As indicated in its GTM strategy, an organization needs to create a comprehensive launch plan for introducing its product(s) to the world. It can achieve this by conducting purposeful meetings with the applicable teams, setting a launch date, and making sure all the necessary procedures are outlined in the plan for a successful launch. To ensure everyone is on board, it is imperative to schedule frequent meetings, evaluate developments, spot obstacles, and make necessary revisions or adjustments to the launch plan. Successful internal milestones, competitive environment, and market conditions should be taken into account while perfecting the launch plan.

Figure 4.2 Product launch steps and timing

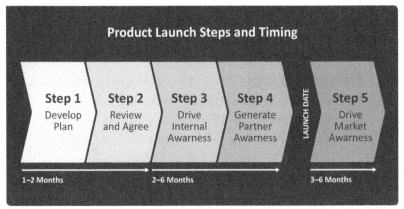

Source: ProductPlan. "How to Create a Product Launch Plan Roadmap." https://www.productplan.com

As demonstrated in Figure 4.2, the product launch steps and timing begin with the development of the launch plan, which is then reviewed and agreed upon by the stakeholders. The next two important steps involve driving awareness internally about the product and reaching out to potential external partners to equally generate additional awareness. It is also important that the internal teams as well as external stakeholders like technology and channel partners be informed and educated about the processes. After that, a date will be selected and agreed upon by the stakeholders for the launching of the product.

It is important to remember all along that the purpose of creating a launch plan is to be able to generate enough excitement and anticipation in consumers when they eventually hear about or see the product. Therefore, organizations need to follow the checklist described below to make their product launch an astounding success.

4.4.1 Product launch plan checklist

The following comprehensive checklist serves as a guide to ensure the key aspects of a product launch are covered throughout the entire launching process.

A. Pre-launch phase

1. **Defining clear objectives:** This entails having a clear outline of goals and objectives in relation to why and when to launch the product and how to measure the success of the launch.
2. **Finalizing the messaging:** An important step in the pre-launch phase is to finalize the messaging for the product and use that for all the assets, blogs, advertisements, websites, internal enablement, and so on. This is covered in greater detail in section 4.5 (collateral building).
3. **Conducting competitive analysis:** Through competitive analysis, an organization can understand its strengths, weaknesses, and how its product stands out among the rivals already on the market.

4. **Building hype and teasers:** Creating anticipation and excitement by generating buzz before the actual launch using teasers, sneak peeks, and countdowns is an effective pre-launch move.

B. <u>Execution phase</u>

5. **Launch event planning:** As much as possible, it is advisable to plan how the launch event will be organized. This could be through a physical or virtual event, webinar, or blog, depending on the target audience and the product to be launched.
6. **Website and landing page optimization:** This entails providing clear product information and ensuring that the landing pages of the company's website are fully optimized for the launch, showing the necessary product benefits and a call-to-action.
7. **Email marketing setup:** One of the proactive steps to take is to set up email campaigns to notify the target audience about the launch, product details, and exclusive offers.
8. **Social media strategy:** The organization's social media handles will be very helpful during this stage. It is important to schedule self-explanatory posts with relevant hashtags to educate the target audience about the new product launch.
9. **PR outreach:** As one of the best practices, it is advisable to provide relevant media outlets, bloggers, and influencers with press releases, product samples, or reviews (if applicable).
10. **Customer support preparation:** At this stage, the customer support team should play a pivotal role in keeping

the audience informed. They are expected to provide excellent customer service and must be ready to handle all questions and inquiries relating to the product launch.

C. Post-launch phase

11. **Monitoring and analytics:** To understand the impact of the product launch, it is important to utilize some analytics tools to track the organization's website traffic, social media engagement, and customer interactions.
12. **Feedback collection:** Collecting feedback from customers and early adopters is quite helpful in determining what improvements or upgrades should be included in the second or succeeding versions of the product. This could also help an organization understand the level of reception for its product in the market.

Based on the customer interest and feedback during the launch, organizations need to adjust their marketing strategies, improve the product, come up with the customer retention plans and build additional content if needed. More details about the post-launch activities are covered in section 4.9 of this chapter.

4.5 Collateral Building

Collateral building in product management and product marketing refers to the process of creating various materials that support the launch, growth, and continuing use of a product.[16] It could also be referred to as any sales or

---

16. Miller, D. (2017). Building a StoryBrand: Clarify Your Message So Customers Will Listen. New York, HarperCollins.

marketing materials that companies employ to advertise their product and services and boost traffic and sales to enhance customer trustworthiness.

4.5.1 Types of collateral:

All the collateral built by Product Marketing and Marketing teams can be divided into 2 types:

1. **Customer facing collateral:**
   - Customer facing collaterals effectively communicate product features and benefits to potential customers.
   - Customer facing collateral include customer facing decks, brochures, case studies, product sheets, articles, e-books, newsletters, blog posts, website content, press releases, social media content, YouTube videos.

2. **Internal collateral:**
   - Internal collateral ensures everyone within the company has a clear understanding of the product and allows salespeople to effectively engage and pitch the product to the customers and partners.
   - Internal collateral include product roadmaps, wireframes, mock-ups, internal training materials, conversation guides, battle cards, FAQ, competitive decks.

4.5.2 Benefits of effective collateral building

- Consistent product messaging, resulting in effectively pitching the product to the end customers

- Improved customer commitment and adoption
- Increased brand awareness and credibility
- Increased sales and traffic conversion

4.5.3 Additional tips

- Collaborate with the marketing, sales, and product marketing teams to ensure that the collateral aligns with the overall GTM strategy and messaging.
- Use data analytics tools to track the effectiveness of different types of collateral employed and adjust your strategies accordingly.
- Regularly update and revise collateral as the product evolves over time.

By following these steps and best practices, product managers can build impactful collateral that supports the success of their products and enhances the user experience.

4.6 Announcement and PR

Announcements and public relations (PR) play a vital role in product management, serving different purposes throughout the product life cycle. Effective utilization of announcements and PR strategies will enable organizations to build positive buzz, attract the right audience, and ultimately contribute to the success of their products. Let's look at their functions:

1. **Product announcements:**
    - **Purpose:** To inform relevant stakeholders about the key product developments and milestones.

- **Some examples of announcements:**
  - New product launch announcements
  - Feature updates and announcements
  - Upcoming product roadmap unveiling
  - Partnerships and integrations
  - Product winning awards and getting recognition from industry experts

2. **Analyst relationships:**
   - **Purpose:** To shape public perception and generate positive press coverage for the product under development.
   - **Target audience:** Primarily focuses on media, influencers, and experts in the field ultimately reaching a broader audience.
   - **Activities:**
     - Develop and maintain relationships with journalists, influencers, industry experts, and bloggers. For B2B products, product managers often connect with industry experts from advisory firms such as Gartner, Forrester, and IDC to educate them about upcoming products, and features.
     - Expert analysts, after hearing about the new product and vision of the company, will share their expert opinions in industry reports and via other mediums with their followers, resulting in more coverage for the product.
     - Participate in industry events, exhibitions, and conferences.

- Manage media inquiries and crisis communication.
- Monitor social media and online conversations to address brand mentions and sentiment.

How product announcements and analyst relationships work together:

- Announcements often form the foundation for analyst relationships.
- Analysts, after hearing about the new product and vision of the company, will share their expert opinions in industry reports and via other mediums with their followers, resulting in more coverage for the product.
- This relationship between the organization and analysts helps the company gain positive media attention, which will help them reach target audiences.

Benefits of effective product announcements and analyst relationships:

- Increased brand awareness and market visibility
- Improved brand reputation and public perception
- Generated excitement and anticipation for new features and launches

Considering analysts and influencers are considered experts in the field, the positive coverage about the product from them increases brand awareness, resulting in increased sales and higher market share in the long run.

4.7 Digital and Social Media Marketing

Figure 4.3 Overview of digital and social media marketing

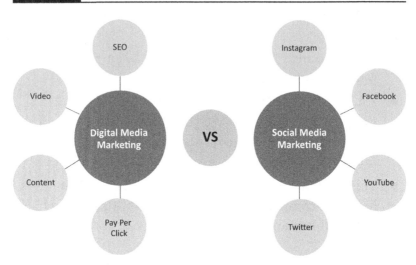

Source: Adapted from Desai, Shamli. "Digital Marketing Vs. Social Media Marketing." *EDUCBA* (blog), November 25, 2022. https://www.educba.com

Digital and social media marketing such as LinkedIn, Facebook, Instagram, TikTok, etc. play a vital role in product management in today's world. Through the smart use of digital and social media marketing, organizations can create a strong brand, connect with their target audience, and ultimately help their products succeed in an already crowded market. An organization can access data to its advantage by utilizing social media platforms and digital marketing tools, which offer useful information on target customers and market trends. When actively engaged on social media, customers can let organizations discover a lot of vital information about them, including their preferences.

Digital and social media platforms may be leveraged to:
- Generate pre-launch buzz and anticipation
- Announce new features and updates to existing users
- Run targeted advertising campaigns to reach potential customers
- Collect user feedback and iterate on the product based on their needs

This would help organizations curate a memorable product launch as well as stimulate user growth.

Organizations use social media and digital platforms to provide a direct line of communication for engaging with clients and fostering partnerships in order to:
- Provide customer support and answer questions
- Gather feedback and address customer concerns proactively
- Build a sense of community and foster user engagement
- Promote user-generated content and testimonials to build trust and credibility

The combination of these strategies will allow an organization to create an all-inclusive marketing approach that aligns with its product goals and target audience. Other areas where social media and digital platforms could be of immense benefit include:

1. **Search engine optimization (SEO):** Implementing SEO strategies on its website will help an organization improve the visibility of its product in search engine results, making it more likely for users to discover its product during random searches on the internet.
2. **Pay-per-click (PPC) advertising:** Running targeted PPC campaigns on platforms like Google Ads or Bing Ads

can drive traffic to an organization's product website and generate leads through paid advertising.

3. **Affiliate marketing:** An organization can utilize a commission-based approach and collaborate with affiliates to market its product on its behalf. This can increase sales and broaden the organization's audience worldwide.

4. **Analytics and data analysis:** Utilizing analytics tools such as Google Analytics, DataDog, and others makes it easier to monitor user activity, assess the success of campaigns, and get information that can be used to improve product offerings and marketing tactics.

5. **Customer engagement:** Through surveys, comments, and messages, social media makes it easier for an organization and its sales/marketing teams to communicate directly with clients, gaining vital input and insights into their preferences and allowing the organization to reach specific demographics.

6. **Community building:** Building and maintaining online communities around its product on sites like LinkedIn groups and Facebook groups will surely help an organization's customers feel more connected to one another and encourage communication and user-generated content related to the product.

4.8 Measuring GTM Success

A Go-To-Market (GTM) strategy's effectiveness is evaluated using a range of metrics that correspond with the objectives established in the planning stage. Through consistent tracking and evaluation of these indicators, an organization may have a thorough grasp of how well its GTM plan has been working. It is advisable that an organization consistently review its success metrics (also known as Key Performance metrics - KPIs) and make adjustments as needed.

The following typical measures may be used to assess how well a particular GTM approach has been performing:

1. **Product launch reach metrics:** When launching a product, even before sales, it is important to discover how many people saw the launch, read the launch blog and article, how many people participated in the free trial, press coverage, and other things. It is equally advisable to monitor website traffic, social media engagement, and attendance at the launch event.
2. **Marketing metrics:**

    - **Lead generation and conversion:** Measuring the effectiveness of marketing strategies employed in generating leads and converting them into free trials and ultimately to paying customers.
    - **Website and social media analytics:** Analyzing website traffic, engagement metrics, and social media performance to assess the effectiveness of the organization's online presence and the possibility of improving its visibility.

3. **Pipeline and sales metrics:**

    - **Marketing qualified leads (MQL) and sales qualified leads (SQL):** One of the key ways to measure the success of the GTM activities is how much pipeline (in dollars) is generated from all the activities. MQL is someone who shows interest in your brand, products, or solutions but may not be ready to make a purchase decision, whereas SQL is someone with buying intent who appears interested in your company's offerings.[17]

- **Conversion rates:** Monitoring the conversion rates at different stages of the sales funnel, from lead generation to final conversion.
- **Sales velocity:** Measuring how quickly leads move through the sales pipeline, providing insights into the efficiency of the sales process.
- **Revenue growth:** In the long term, it is important to track and compare the overall increase in revenue generated before the pre-launch and after the product launch.

4. **Adaptation and learning metrics:**

   - **Key learnings and adjustments:** It is important for an organization to document its key learning points or observations from the GTM strategy, using the obtained insights to make adjustments and improvements for future reference.
   - **Market feedback and trends:** Staying informed about market trends and gathering continuous feedback from customers to adapt GTM strategy and offerings accordingly.

5. **Choosing the right metrics:**

   - The specific metrics an organization chooses will depend on its unique goals, product category, and business model.

---

17. Rollworks (2024). MQL vs. SQL: A Guide to Maximizing Revenue Growth. Available at: https://www.rollworks.com

- It is advisable not to rely solely on any single metric as a definitive measure of GTM success; as a matter of fact, the combination of a few metrics will do the magic. It is also advisable to analyze trends and combine data from different sources to gain a holistic view of GTM activity's performance.

4.9 Post-Launch Activities

To ensure continuous success and progression of its product after it has been introduced to the market, the next essential part of a GTM effort is to conduct post-launch activities, which focus on customer support, customer feedback, optimization, and ongoing marketing efforts.[18]

Listed are some of the post-launch activities that an organization should consider undertaking:[19]

1. **Customer support and engagement:**

   - **Customer support channels:** The organization's teams must promptly respond to customers' questions and complaints by using a variety of channels, including phone, email, and live support.
   - **FAQs and knowledge base:** The organization must frequently update its Frequently Asked Questions (FAQs) and also ensure to provide regular updates on all other knowledge-based materials.
   - **User community management:** Promoting and interacting with user groups or discussion boards, using some of its dedicated team members to help people

---

18. Sekaran, S. (2020). Product Marketing, Simplified: A Customer-Centric Approach to Take a Product to Market. Seattle, Amazon.
19. Turayhi S.,. *The Launch: A Product Marketer's Guide: 50 Key Questions & Lessons for A Successful Launch.* (Seattle: Amazon, 2021), 28-60

feel like they share in the organization's vision/ mission and to stimulate conversations.

2. **Feedback collection and analysis:**

    - **Customer surveys:** Conducting customer surveys to obtain input on the product, user experience, and potential areas for enhancement.
    - **User reviews and testimonials:** Encouraging consumers to provide reviews and testimonials and keeping an eye on and replying to comments on many platforms.
    - **Social media listening:** Keeping an eye out on social media platforms for mentions and comments about the product, and quickly resolving any problems or worries that may arise.

It is important to assess the product launch's overall success by taking lessons learned and key performance indicators into account as well as encouraging the team members that participated in the product launch to provide feedback and learn from their experiences.

3. **Marketing and promotion:**

    - To keep its customers interested in its product, an organization should keep producing and disseminating insightful materials/content about its product, new features, market trends, and customer success stories.
    - Sending out customized email marketing campaigns to educate clients about upcoming deals, new features, and pertinent information.

- Engaging with its audience on social media by posting updates and customer success stories and by being active on these channels 24/7.

4. **Customer retention strategies:**

    - Employing loyalty programs or special offers on a regular basis can serve as a means of incentivizing repeat purchases and rewarding loyal customers.
    - Developing campaigns that offer complementary items or premium features to current consumers in order to cross-sell and upsell.
    - Utilizing insights derived from data to tailor offers and communications to the unique interests and actions of each consumer. This is because customers see and react to things differently.

Chapter Summary

- Every organization is required to have a clear Go-To-Market (GTM) Strategy to effectively communicate its value and product differentiation to end customers.

- GTM begins with understanding its customers' product buying cycles and positioning the product that will explain the unique value proposition of the product and eventually, encourage the purchase of the product.

- A launch plan is a document that details all the necessary steps an organization needs to take in order to successfully launch its new product.

- For an organization to get its messages to its current and prospective customers, a combination of approaches are required, including creating a sales/marketing collateral and making product announcements by utilizing PR, digital, and social media marketing.

- At the end of these processes, it is essential to measure the effectiveness of the GTM Strategy and modify it as needed to ensure product success in the long run.

Quiz

1. The three main components of an effective Go-To-Market (GTM) Strategy are....
   a. Customer, pricing, and business plan
   b. Target market profiles, marketing plan, and distribution strategy
   c. Business plan, sales, plan, and marketing plan

2. It is imperative for organizations to finalize their product messaging during the pre-launch stage so that they can use the same messaging in their advertisements, blogs, websites, and other assets.
   a. False
   b. True

3. The process of partnering with influencers or content creators to promote and sell products directly to their engaged audience is referred to as....
   a. Marketplace integration
   b. Influencer collaboration
   c. Digital marketing

4. A product's positioning is all about outlining its....
   a. Unique selling propositions
   b. Packaging type
   c. Texture

5. Why is it important for organizations to fully "know their stories" while pitching their new products to consumers?
   a. To be able to showcase their products' good benefits to consumers
   b. To cajole consumers into buying their products
   c. To force their products on unsuspicious consumers

6. A great positioning message should be all of these except being....
   a. Deceptive
   b. Clear
   c. Memorable

7. The product buying cycle can also be referred to as the...
   a. Sales and marketing cycle
   b. Product roadmap
   c. Go-to-market plan

8. There are intrinsically — stages in the product buying cycle.
   a. 5
   b. 4
   c. 3

9. At what stage do consumers finally make up their minds to buy a product?
   a. Awareness stage
   b. Purchase stage
   c. Decision stage

10. Which of these activities does not occur during a product's pre-launch phase?
    a. Target audience identification
    b. Competitive analysis
    c. Feedback collection

Answers

1 – b	2 – b	3 – b	4 – a	5 – a
6 – a	7 – a	8 – b	9 – b	10 – c

CHAPTER 5
After the First Product Launch

Key Learning Objectives

- Measuring success
- Customer feedback loop and product lifecycle
- Win-loss analysis and funnel analysis
- Portfolio planning
- The implications of lifetime value of the customer

The first product launch is a step in making the product available to those who want it. After that, most organizations would build sales momentum for their products by setting up helpful customer service, answering any complaints and questions customers may have, and offering the necessary assistance that would help consumers derive much benefit from using the product. At this stage, customers' feedback is crucial to ensure the product can be improved for future iterations.

5.1 Measuring Success

Before the product is launched, it is important to identify the ultimate goal of the product (also called as north star metrics) so that we can measure the success of the product once the product is launched. Please note that the north star of the product can change as the product goes through different stages of the product life cycle.

Once the product is launched, the organizations need to measure whether the launch achieved the goals/targets expected prior to the launch of the product. In business terms, these goals are called key performance indicators (KPIs).

5.1.1 Measuring success pre-production or before general availability (GA)

It is essential to understand that no product becomes widely adopted right after its development. It goes through a series of iterations before it gains appreciable traction in the market. In the meantime, right after a product is launched, product managers want credible answers to these pertinent questions:

1. **How many customers tried the product?** — Product managers need to understand how many customers are interested in the product. Some organizations often share early versions of the new product with their existing customers for trials to obtain some useful feedback from them.

2. **How many are considering buying or interested in the product?** — Based on the initial feedback garnered from the testers and trials conducted by the customers, is there any significant interest in buying the product? There is a difference between liking to have a product

and actually buying it and hence, product managers need to identify whether the product is good to have or must have for the customers and understand the propensity to buy the product.

3. **Did they use all the product's features?** — Among those who have genuinely expressed interest in purchasing the product, what do they think about the product's functionality? Did they use all its available features? Did they think the product was useful enough the way it was and ready for production environment use?

If customers' responses to the three technical questions above were positive, that could indicate that the product holds some promise of doing well when it is released to the market.

After the initial launch phase, as more customers start using the product, it is important to track how engaged customers are and whether they use the product once and never return or they come back frequently and use the product on a regular basis. In the case of software products, to fully understand how visitors are engaged and retained, it is helpful to investigate their daily active sessions (DAU) and monthly active sessions (MAU). What motivated them to sign up? Did they sign up because the offering was free or because it had an advanced feature they liked? How many times did they visit the product page before finally deciding to sign up? Were they motivated by the discounts or coupons offered before signing up? For those who didn't sign up on their first visit, how many visits did they make before eventually signing up? Those who left and did not complete their signing up, did they encounter any error while signing up? It is important to find pertinent answers to the above-stated questions to improve the signup workflow.

During this stage, it is also important to measure other stats such as bounce rates, session duration, social media engagement, loyalty, recency, and the depth of the visit among others.

It is also important to track how the customer acquisition cost is related to how the visitors find out about the product. Did they come to the organization's product page through search, organic traffic, direct, referrals, or via ads?

5.1.2 Measuring success: How the metrics change along a product life cycle

In its lifecycle, a product typically goes through different stages. More importantly, the metrics required to measure success also change along the line.

- **Development stage:** The most important metrics at this stage include those that measure time to market, meeting budget, and achieving pre-planned milestones.
- **Launch stage:** During this stage, user acquisition, customer's propensity to buy the product, and customer feedback top the list of useful metrics.
- **Growth stage:** Metrics that measure revenue growth, customer retention, and market share are given more consideration at this stage.
- **Maturity stage:** When a product is doing well in the market, having been widely adopted by consumers, it is time to analyze metrics that estimate profit margins, customer satisfaction and market share.
- **Decline stage:** At this stage, it is imperative to measure sales decline, customer churn, and pay attention to cost efficiency.

5.2 Customer Feedback Loop

A customer feedback loop is a continuous process of accumulating, analyzing, and acting upon customer feedback to improve products and services to improve customer satisfaction. When an organization's feedback loop is robust enough, it will proactively handle customers' needs/requirements and address their concerns.[20] There is no magic to achieving an excellent customer feedback loop except that it should be refined over time to ensure its effectiveness in delivering meaningful insights and driving product roadmap to increase customer satisfaction and targeting new customer segments.

Here's a breakdown of the key elements in a typical customer feedback loop that any organization and their PMs can implement:

1. **Collecting customer feedback:**

    - Create and disseminate surveys or questionnaires to get organized input on particular aspects of client's experiences.
    - Use feedback forms at physical touchpoints such as retail stores, point of sale (POS), events and exhibitions, etc., on websites, or in applications, to get honest and direct input from customers or via one-on-one customer conversations on Zoom, conferences, partner events, and other avenues.
    - Record customer behavior through tools such as Tableau, Google Analytics, and others. This

---

20. Markey, R., Reichheld, F., Dullweber, A. (2009). Closing the Customer Feedback Loop. *Harvard Business Review*. Available at: https://hbr.org/2009/12/closing-the-customer-feedback-loop Accessed 5 March 2024.

helps product managers understand the customer behavior for the product.

- Keep an eye out on social media channels for any mentions, messages, or comments pertaining to the brand in order to get immediate feedback.
- Encourage clients to post reviews on review sites related to the organization's industry or sector or on sites like Bing, Ask, Google, or other search engines.
- Record both good and negative feedback from customers in order to spot patterns and areas that need to be improved.

2. **Analyzing and organizing feedback:**

- Sort reviews according to categories such as features of the product, customer support, cost, and overall contentment. Once the product manager has collected the feedback, it will be analyzed and incorporated into the roadmap so that the product can be further improved.
- Employ sentiment analysis methods to distinguish between positive, negative, and neutral feelings in customer feedback.
- Examine quantitative metrics such as customer satisfaction, customer effort score, and net promoter score.
- Determine recurrent patterns in customers' comments to help prioritize the areas that need further improvement.
- Analyze the feedback and incorporate that into the roadmap so that the product can be improved further, as necessary.

3. **Implementing changes and improvements:**

    - Obtain valuable information from consumer feedback and utilize it to guide strategic choices and enhance operational efficiency.
    - Execute essential changes based on feedback and facilitate communication across various departments such as product, marketing, and customer care.
    - Prioritize both short-term successes and long-term objectives based on client input, fixing urgent issues, and making plans for long-term improvements. This may involve adding the new features to the roadmap and prioritizing them based on the urgency and revenue impact.

4. **Closing the loop with customers:**

    - Close the deal with clients by keeping them updated on developments, thanking them for their input, and sending them follow-up correspondence.
    - Maintain open communication by immediately responding to clients using the platforms they used to provide feedback, such as social media or email.
    - Establish discussion boards or communities where clients can exchange ideas, communicate with the brand and one another, and debate feedback.

5. **About the iterative process:**

    - Track consumer feedback over time to spot changing patterns and areas that could need constant attention.
    - Periodically analyze the gathered feedback data to evaluate the success of improvements that have been put into place and find other areas that need improvement.

5.3 Understanding the Product Lifecycle

As covered earlier, a product goes through several phases, including the introduction phase when it was first launched, followed by the growth phase, the maturity stage, and finally the decline stage. These product stages are collectively referred to as the product life cycle. To make wise judgments about marketing tactics, resource allocation, pricing, and other aspects of the product, organizations must have a thorough understanding of their products' lifecycles.

| Figure 5.1 | A product life cycle |

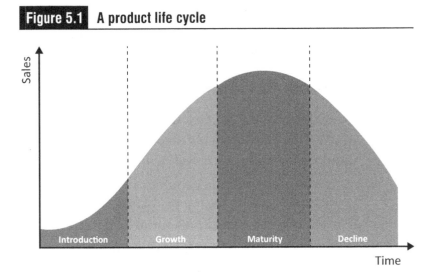

Source: Adapted from Sraders, Anne. "What Is the Product Life Cycle? Stages and Examples." TheStreet, October 29, 2021. https://www.thestreet.com

Organizations that successfully manage each phase of their products' life cycles can consequently improve the success of their products, sustain their growth and demand, and maintain their positions as market leaders.

A typical product lifetime consists of the following 4 essential stages:

1. **Market introduction:** Newly developed products face the challenge of low sales and limited market awareness. In order to establish market presence, and generate awareness and curiosity, it is imperative to massively market the new product. It is advisable to focus on the needs of the early adopters to make sure the product is successful. Organizations can decide to make limited versions of their products (applies to hardware products) at this stage to avoid wasting scarce resources on mass-producing products that they are not sure will be widely accepted by consumers. At this stage, testing and iterating the product helps the organization learn quickly from the customers and reduce risks. The main objective of the market introduction is to achieve product-market fit, which means the product substantially satisfies the problems of the target customers. Once the product-market fit is achieved, the product can move to the next phase in the product life cycle which is a growth phase.

2. **Growth:** Once the product achieves the product market fit, it is the right time for organizations to increase the production in the case of hardware products. For software products, once the product gets into a growth phase, the product managers focus on delivering additional functionalities to increase adoption and ultimately increase the revenue. At this stage it may be sensible to test the market with different versions of the product and release them to the market via various distribution channels. To achieve significant product growth, organizations may optimize their existing products by adding more useful features and focus on differentiating their product from other solutions in the market to increase their market share.

At this stage, organizations also concentrate on getting to profitability as soon as possible. This may require providing additional features for mainstream appeal, and expanding and optimizing sales channels while keeping an eye on competitors.

3. **Maturity:** Sooner or later, most of the products reach the maturity stage irrespective of how great and useful they are. At their maturity stage, every product's sales volume peaks, due to the fact that the product has already saturated the market and competitors in the market have more or less the same product. During this phase, organizations have to keep reinforcing the product differentiation to the customers to retain and possibly steal the market share from other players in the market. It may be advisable to reduce prices as well as carrying out market diversification—which entails that the product could be sold somewhere else. The primary objectives for most organizations at this stage are to maximize profit and extend their product lifetime. In order to achieve those goals, it is important that they differentiate their products from all alternatives in the market, add adjacent products or segments to their product line(s), and make an attempt to expand their reach through acquisitions and targeting new geography to sell the product.

4. **Decline:** When a product reaches the decline phase, it means its sales are starting to slide down, probably because consumers have found newer alternatives to solve their problems. To manage their products' decline, organizations need to take some strategic steps such as reducing the prices of their products or cutting their losses by discontinuing the manufacturing of the

declined products. For example, when people started watching movies and listening to music online at websites such as YouTube, Netflix, and other platforms, it resulted in the decline of CD players.

In the decline stage, the company may work on transitioning their customers from one of their products to another. Some of their priorities during this period may include eliminating unnecessary investment or cost and partnering with other businesses or repackaging their products. If everything else fails, the last sensible move will be to allow their product to exit the market gracefully.

Figure 5.2 summarizes the objectives and priorities in each stage of the product life cycle.

Figure 5.2 The product life cycle

Source: PRINCIPLES OF MARKETING. "Product Life Cycle Stages & Strategies," December 19, 2014. https://somartinblog.wordpress.com

5.4 Win-Loss Analysis and Funnel Analysis

Organizations can employ techniques such as funnel analysis and win-loss analysis to understand customer behavior and figure out ways to improve product adoption. While funnel analysis helps optimize the entire sales process and offers a larger perspective on the customer journey, win-loss analysis delivers insights into specific sales prospects. Let's examine each in detail.

5.4.1 Win-loss analysis

A **win-loss analysis** is a process where organizations systematically evaluate the reasons behind both successful (win) and unsuccessful (loss) sales opportunities. It involves understanding the factors that contributed to winning a deal as well as those that led to losing a deal.

Key components of a win-loss analysis

- **Interviewing customers or internal stakeholders:** To obtain firsthand information, an organization's marketing team or product manager needs to speak with both won and lost consumers. The aim of the process is to better understand customer purchasing criteria, viewpoints, and decision-making processes. If it is not possible to talk to the customers, the product managers can talk to the account teams and other folks who worked on the deal to gather relevant information on why we won or lost the deal.
- **Data collection:** The product manager or the marketing team needs to gather quantitative information on competitive positioning, product attributes, and price for both gained and lost prospects.

- **Analysis and patterns:** The gathered information should be examined to find trends, patterns, and similarities between different won and lost deals.
- **Report and suggestions:** A thorough report with actionable suggestions for enhancing product's featureset, positioning, sales tactics, and overall competitiveness should be prepared from the collected data. This can be used to further improve the roadmap, product positioning or simplify the product journey for the customer with the goal of converting the lost deals into won deals in the future.

The benefits of win-loss analysis

- **Insights into customer decision-making:** Organizations can gain insights into how customers make decisions by knowing what factors lead them to winning or losing the deal.
- **Product improvement:** Feedback gathered from the win-loss analysis can guide the roadmap so that the product can be improved over time to improve the win rate and increase revenue.
- **Competitive intelligence:** Useful knowledge about the strengths and weaknesses of an organization's rivals can be obtained via the win-loss analysis so as to better position itself in the market.
- **Continual improvement:** With this analysis, it is possible to create a feedback loop to help sales and marketing initiatives get better over time.

5.4.2 Funnel analysis

Funnel analysis is a useful technique for understanding the actual steps taken by a customer before taking a final action, such as purchasing the product. Let's take an e-commerce website for example. Funnel analysis will reveal exactly where the drop-offs occur or where the consumers decided not to complete their purchases. It is possible to analyze the factors causing drop-offs with the hope of designing a workflow to improve consumers' purchasing journey or experience.

Figure 5.3 Using funnel analysis to improve customer journeys

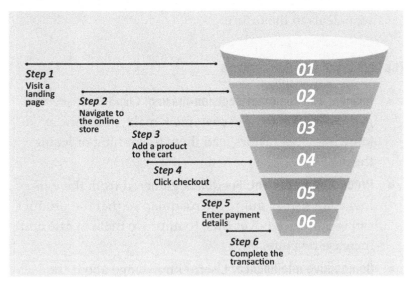

Source: Adapted from Olmstead, Levi. "What Is Funnel Analysis? +Benefits, Examples, Tools." *The Whatfix Blog | Drive Digital Adoption* (blog), November 3, 2022. https://whatfix.com

Figure 5.3 reveals the series of steps taken by a consumer while navigating to buy something from an e-commerce store. Before customers make any buying decisions, they will go through the following steps:

Step 1: Visit the landing page of the brand where the information about the product is available.

Step 2: Navigate to the online store to possibly learn more about the product's features, attributes, and usefulness.

Step 3: Add a desirable product to the cart.

Step 4: Click checkout to buy it.

Step 5: Enter the payment details such as the credit card numbers, address, phone number, and other pieces of information required by the seller.

Step 6: The purchase is completed.

Key components of the funnel analysis:

- **Defining funnel stages:** Identify and define the important phases of the customer journey. In the case of e-commerce websites such as Amazon, the funnel stages could be customer sign-up, customer login, browsing items/check reviews, adding the product to the cart, making a purchase, and then adding a review for the product.
- **Data collection:** Compile information on customer interactions and behaviors at every stage of the funnel, frequently using analytics platforms such as Google Analytics, Data Dog, and others.
- **Conversion metrics:** Monitor conversion metrics at every stage to gauge the success of the product's ease of use, marketing, and sales initiatives.
- **Identifying drop-offs:** Locate any snags or drop-offs in the funnel where potential customers are lost and investigate the causes of these drop-offs. Drop-offs occur when a consumer decides not to go to the next stage of the funnel.
- **Identifying opportunities for improvement:** Determine which parts of the funnel require fine-tuning and create plans to improve the flow of customers' buying patterns.

- **Conversion rate optimization:** Provided the enhancements we identified in the previous steps are correct, the improvements should enhance the conversion rates and improve the customer journey, leading to improved conversation (i.e. the final purchase in the case of e-commerce websites).

5.5 Portfolio Planning

A company's product portfolio refers to the range of products and services offered to customers. It is important that companies actively diversify their product portfolios to sustain the business through shifting market scenarios and changing customer preferences. For small and medium-sized companies that possess a few products, portfolio planning can be an easy task. However, it is exceedingly complex for large corporations with a diverse and large number of products/services to manage or plan their product portfolio.

In principle, portfolio planning allows the organization to develop complementary products that can be sold as a package or separately. Another way to expand to the new product area is to engage in mergers and acquisitions (M&As) to take over businesses that are producing their desirable products. In the tech world, it is often difficult for startups to compete at a global scale with big companies and so, we more often see big players acquiring smaller companies and startups to expand their portfolio rather than investing on research and development to launch a new product. Facebook acquiring Instagram and Google acquiring Youtube can be considered as some of the most successful acquisitions done by the big companies to expand their portfolios.

A product portfolio strategy is a company's plan on how to increase its market share and enter a new area of business that might be solving additional problems for existing customers or building the product for new customer segments.

To successfully develop a product portfolio strategy and identify areas of growth and expansion, an organization needs to conduct a comprehensive list of analyses, including customer research, competitor research, BCG growth-share matrix, and SWOT Analysis among others. Please note that the BCG growth-share matrix and SWOT analysis will be covered in great detail in Chapter Eight of this book.

Organizations can take two basic paths to expand their product portfolio:

- **Incremental growth:** This approach entails increasing the market share steadily and slowly without spending a lot of its resources. The company doesn't need to spend so much money on creating a new product line and instead focuses on enhancing existing products to increase the market share. A simple example of incremental growth would be Amazon starting as an online bookstore but later on expanding to other product areas such as toys, clothes, household essentials etc. to increase its market share.
- **Disruptive growth:** On the other hand, an organization may want to strategically expand its market reach by investing heavily on creating a new product line or acquiring new products through mergers and acquisitions. Disruptive growth usually happens externally, and it may come at a huge cost. An example for the disruptive growth would be Amazon starting as an online bookstore but later on launching Amazon Web Service (AWS) that was a completely new service

that targeted a completely new customer segment and disrupted the entire cloud computing industry.

5.6 Lifetime Value of the Customer

Customer Lifetime Value (CLV) is a critical metric used by organizations to evaluate the total value that a customer is expected to generate over the course of their relationship with them. This important metric, which is also referred to as Customer LTV, is helpful to organizations because it gives them a clear picture of how much they can generate per customer account. This will assist them in making well-informed decisions about marketing, customer acquisition, and sales.

5.6.1 Understanding customer lifetime value

For any organization to correctly determine its CLV, the following parameters must be taken into consideration:

- **Revenue contribution:** Customer Lifetime Value (CLV) doesn't only estimate revenue contribution from customers' single purchases, but it also considers their future purchases and subscriptions to additional services.
- **Importance of retention:** There is a direct correlation between customer retention and customer lifetime value. Any organization with strong customer retention tends to have exceedingly high CLV.
- **Marketing efficiency:** Organizations that understand the positive implication of high CLV will invest heavily in their marketing efforts to acquire and retain long-term, high-value customers.

- **Customer segmentation:** Organizations can use information or data about their high-value customer segments to expand in that segment even further.
- **Profitability indicator:** If the organization's ongoing Customer Acquisition Cost (CAC) and other servicing costs are lower than its overall CLV, it reveals that the organization is enjoying a profitable relationship with its customers.[21]

5.6.2 Calculating customer lifetime value

The customer lifetime value can be estimated using this simple formula:

=**Annual profit contribution per customer × Average number of years that they remain a customer**

For instance, **if the profit generated by the customer each year** = $2,000

Number of years that they are a customer of the brand = 4 years

And the cost to acquire the customer = $1,000

The customer lifetime value (CLV) of this customer = $2,000 (annual profit from the customer) × 4 (number of years that they are a customer) - $1,000 (acquisition cost) = $7,000

With additional parameters such as the ones provided below, it is possible to calculate CLV using the simple formula above:

If the annual revenue per average customer = $3,000 per annum

The product costs associated with the average customer's purchases = $400 per year

---

21. Kumar, V. (2008). Customer Lifetime Value: The Path to Profitability. Norwell, Massachusetts.

If the company also spends $200 a year per customer to provide customer service

And the annual retention rate (loyalty rate) = 80%

The average costs to acquire a new customer = $2,000

First, let **calculate the average annual profit per customer** = annual revenue - product costs - service costs) = 3000 − 400 − 200 = $2400 (**profit**)

Since, the number of years the customer has been with the company is not given, but we have the annual retention rate (loyalty rate) of the customer, which is 80%, we can convert the customer's retention rate to his lifetime period with the company.

We can use either:

100% divided by (100% minus **the annual retention rate**)

OR

(1 / 1- annual retention rate)

Since we are working with an 80% loyalty rate, the average customer lifetime can be calculated thus:

100% / (100% − 80%) =

100% / 20% = **5 years average customer lifetime period**

Having all the necessary parameters to calculate CLV, therefore CLV = $2,400 (profit) × 5 (years) − $2,000 (acquisition) = $10,000

5.6.3 Interpreting CLV

- **Positive CLV:** This reveals a positive customer relationship between an organization and its customers whereby the overall customer value exceeds the costs incurred in acquiring and retaining them.

- **Negative CLV:** This indicates that the organization is spending more on acquiring and retaining customers than the income (or revenue) it is getting from them. This may cause the organization to review and revise its business plan.
- **Increasing CLV:** Organizations can strategically increase their CLV by improving their products and marketing approaches, targeting high-value, long-term customers, and upselling additional and related products that the customers might be interested in.
- **Customer segmentation opportunities:** Using the insights provided by the CLV, organizations can identify the high-value customer segments and focus on retaining them with streamlined customer service and building more complimentary products that appeal to high-value customer segments.

5.6.4 Factors influencing CLV

The following are some essential factors influencing CLV:

- **Customer retention:** In principle, long-term customers give an organization a better CLV, because the longer they patronize the organization, the more they spend on its products.
- **Average transaction value:** When the average amount customers spend on the organization's product rises, the CLV automatically increases. The average profit per transaction may also contribute to higher CLV.
- **Purchase frequency:** When the rate of customers' purchases increases, the CLV correspondingly goes up.

- **Customer Acquisition Costs (CAC):** When organizations succeed in lowering the costs of acquiring and retaining new customers, they can strategically increase the overall CLV.
- **Churn rate:** By lowering the number of dissatisfied customers who stop doing business with an organization, the company can systematically increase its CLV. Retaining high-value customers in the long term will have a positive impact on CLV.
- **Upselling and cross-selling:** It is possible for the existing customers of an organization to show genuine interest in other products/services offered by the organization. However, it requires strategic upselling and cross-selling to introduce those additional products to them.

Chapter Summary

- We need to measure KPIs to understand the success of the product launch.
- Customer feedback loop gives organizations the unique opportunity to obtain feedback about the launched product to incorporate it into the product roadmap as well as improve marketing activities.
- Organizations pay serious attention to their products' life cycles to better manage their viability and marketability, and to maximize the revenue they can generate from the product.
- Win-loss equips an organization with useful information about why the product is winning or losing in the market so that the product can be improved in the long run.
- Funnel analysis is a useful technique for understanding the actual steps taken by a customer before taking a final definite action (for example - purchasing a product on the e-commerce website.)
- Every organization dreams of having customers with a high degree of Customer Lifetime Value because it means they will continue to patronize the organization's products for a very long time.
- For any organization to achieve a very high CLV, it must reduce churn rate, segment high-value customers, upsell and cross-sell its products, and offer excellent customer service to its existing and prospective customers.

Quiz

1. Funnel analysis is a useful technique for understanding the actual steps taken by a customer before taking a final purchasing action.
   a. False
   b. True

2. The sales team estimates a campaign's bounce rate, session duration, or users' interactions with the product. All these parameters are referred to as....
   a. Qualitative metrics
   b. Engagement metrics
   c. Quantitative metrics

3. .... can be defined as a continuous process of accumulating, analyzing, and acting upon customer feedback that can be used to improve an organization's products or services.
   a. Messaging position
   b. Customer feedback loop
   c. Competitive analysis

4. Sentiment analysis can help organizations to distinguish between positive, negative, and neutral feelings in customer feedback.
   a. False
   b. True

5. One of the best practices in any industry is to gather consumer feedback and utilize it to guide strategic business choices and enhance operational efficiency.
   a. True
   b. False

6. How many stages does a typical product life cycle consist of?
   a. 5
   b. 3
   c. 4

7. The last stage in the product life cycle is known as the... stage.
   a. Maturity
   b. Decline
   c. Growth

8. Why is it necessary for organizations to adapt their product prices to each stage in their product life cycles?
   a. To reduce the costs of marketing
   b. To lower their growth rates
   c. To put their customers' perceptions and competitors into consideration

9. .... is a process where organizations systematically evaluate the reasons behind both successful (win) and unsuccessful (loss) sales opportunities.
   a. Funnel analysis
   b. Win-loss analysis
   c. Competitor analysis

10. .....is the process of following and examining a customer's journey from first awareness to last conversion.
   a. Market analysis
   b. Win-loss analysis
   c. Funnel analysis

Answers

1 – b	2 – b	3 – b	4 – b	5 – a
6 – c	7 – b	8 – c	9 – b	10 – c

CHAPTER 6
Skills Needed to Become A Top-Tier Product Manager

Key Learning Objectives
- Key product management skills, namely customer empathy, communication, tech/domain knowledge, leading without authority, business acumen, relationship management, negotiation, attention to details, and data analysis
- The strategic significance of each of these skills

Product managers come from various backgrounds including engineering, tech support, sales, business consulting, and MBA to name a few. While customer empathy and communication are a few basic soft-skills for product managers to understand customer issues and solve them innovatively, PMs need a lot of other skills to become successful in their role. This chapter lists down the various skills needed to become a top-tier product manager and the strategic significance gained by mastering each of these skills.

6.1 Customer Empathy

It is the product manager's responsibility to build the product and features that make the customer's life easy. To solve the right problems for the customers, it is imperative that the PM understands customer problems deeply before coming up with innovative solutions to solve the problems.

Product managers who genuinely develop customer empathy are able to build products and solutions that improve the lives of their customers. Consistently solving the core pain points and use cases for the customers allows the organization to build products that generate consistent revenue for the organization.

6.1.1 How to develop customer empathy

The simplest way to gain customer empathy is to talk to as many customers as possible to better understand their goals, how they currently use the product, and what are the biggest challenges they face while using the product. Based on these customer conversations, the next step is to build buyer and user persona as covered in section 2.6. The customer conversations can happen 1:1 or in a group. Organizations regularly schedule Customer Advisory Board (CAB) sessions to hear from their top customers so that they have the opportunity to learn about customer pain points and use cases. Attending the events that your customers attend is also a great opportunity to connect with your customers and learn from them.

Another way to gain customer empathy is to deeply analyze the customer behavior data to build hypotheses on how customers use the product and identify areas of improvement. Funnel analysis covered in Chapter Five can help with a better understanding of customer behavior.

6.2 Communication

As shown in Figure 6.1, the role of the product manager is at the intersection of customer, technology, and business. To ensure the entire organization is aligned with the product vision and plans, it is imperative for the product manager to be able to communicate with stakeholders from different backgrounds and departments. Communication is a key soft skill every product manager must possess.

Figure 6.1 A product manager's role

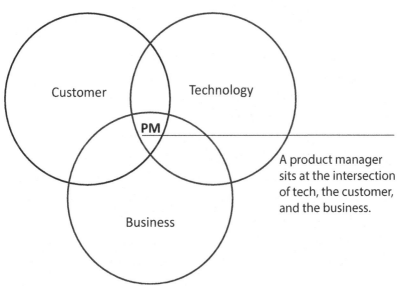

A product manager sits at the intersection of tech, the customer, and the business.

Source: Atlassian. "Product Manager: The Role and Best Practices for Beginners." Atlassian. https://www.atlassian.com

6.2.1 The significance of communication in product management

1. **Aligning teams:** Product managers work cross-functionally across engineering, design, marketing, strategy, and other departments. While communicating with different departments, product managers need to clearly communicate the vision of the product in the language that different departments understand to ensure cross-functional alignment and focus on the same objective across all departments.

2. **Getting buy-in for the vision:** Coming up with ideas to improve the product is just the starting point. Product managers are required to get the buy-in from upper management and stakeholders before conceptualizing the product and setting the vision. Product managers need to rely on oral and written communication, along with visual presentations to champion the idea of a new product with the cross-functional teams and get the buy-in from the upper management and stakeholders. If stakeholders are not confident about the viability of the product that the product manager is pitching, they will not be supportive of such ideas. Good communication skills are mandatory to get the buy-in for the new product idea not only from upper management but other departments as well.

3. **Storytelling and presentations:** Once the product vision is established and the engineering team starts building the product, the product manager collaborates with the product marketing team to create the product positioning and educate the sales team so that they can narrate the product vision and capabilities to the customers. When narrating the product vision

and capabilities to the sales team and customers, the product manager has to rely on the power of oration and presentation skills to educate the audience in a limited time.

4. **Conflict resolution:** Considering the product manager works cross-functionally with so many departments, managing conflicts and disagreements between different departments and stakeholders is one of the primary responsibilities of a product manager. Active listening is necessary to understand the disagreements between different stakeholders and after that, the product manager needs to effectively communicate to resolve the conflict and create a win-win situation so that different departments are aligned on the product vision and execution plans.

6.3 Tech/Domain Knowledge

In the highly competitive field of product management, having a thorough understanding of technology and domain knowledge is not only advantageous but also necessary for individuals hoping to be placed in the top 10% caliber. More importantly, it also allows product managers to understand/empathize with their customers' pain points and use cases. Domain knowledge is also needed to better understand how different players in the market are positioning and building the products so that product managers can come up with a unique way to solve the customer problems and differentiate their product in the market.

6.3.1 Significance of tech/domain knowledge

1. **Enabling knowledge-based decision-making:** Product managers can make wise decisions when they have a firm understanding of the nuances of technology and domain expertise in their respective industries. It also allows them to understand strategies of different players in the domain and come up with a unique way of solving customer problems. Strong technical plus domain knowledge becomes the cornerstone for making strategic decisions, whether assessing technical viability or comprehending market dynamics.

2. **Catalyst for innovation:** Domain and deep tech expertise stimulates innovation. It enables product managers to collaborate with the engineering team to build effective solutions for the customer problems, thus satisfying market demands.

3. **Continuous learning:** It is advisable for product managers to keep up with the latest tech trends and new developments in their fields or industries by updating their knowledge on emerging technologies on a regular basis. They also need to recognize the changing dynamics of their industries while staying current with the market trends and competition.

4. **Proficiency in multiple functions:** Product managers are expected to establish a bridge between technical and non-technical teams by efficiently communicating with them, converting technical specifications into business goals and vice versa. Tech and domain expertise becomes useful to carry out this responsibility.

5. **Hands-on experience:** It is important for product managers to get practical knowledge about the technical aspects of product development by gaining hands-on experience with prototyping and testing tools.
6. **Customer-centric tech application:** In essence, product managers should use their technical expertise to match product features to user requirements, making sure that technology facilitates improved user experiences. This entails that product managers utilize their domain/technical expertise to recognize and creatively address user problems that balance technical viability and user appeal.

6.4 Leading Without Authority

Product managers don't have the formal authority over engineering and other teams within the organization yet product managers have to guide and persuade cross-functional teams towards a product vision and decision-making by building strong relationships, presenting compelling data, and effectively communicating the product's value proposition to stakeholders, all while actively listening and understanding different perspectives. Gaining proficiency in leading without authority is essential for individuals who want to rank among top product managers.

Top-tier product managers are distinguished by their deliberate approach to leadership without authority, which is not an innate talent. A product's success and, by extension, a product manager's career path, depend heavily on their ability to lead teams toward a common goal, without exercising harsh and oppressive authority.

Figure 6.2   six ways to influence without authority

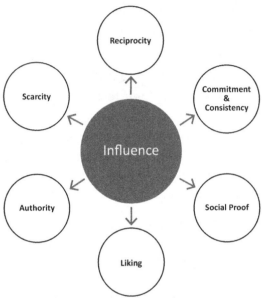

Source: Adapted from Institute of Product Leadership. "Five Ways to Influence without Authority," February 18, 2014. https://www.productleadership.com

In addition to their statutory authority by virtue of their position, Figure 6.2 indicates that product managers can equally exercise some level of influence on teams within their organizations as well as on external stakeholders by utilizing various attributes such as being likeable, demonstrating commitment to their organizations' goals, convincing external stakeholders with their organizations' social proofs, and creating temporary scarcity to create genuine interest in their organizations' products.

6.4.1 The strategic significance of leading without authority

1. **Cross-functional collaboration:** An essential component of cross-functional collaboration is leadership without authority. Product managers frequently collaborate with teams of engineers, designers, and marketers over whom they do not have direct control. Being able to lead without official authority promotes alignment and cooperation.
2. **Influencing decision-making:** Even in situations where they don't have the last word, outstanding product managers are adept at influencing decisions. This ability is crucial for determining the course of products, winning people over to ideas, and bringing disparate viewpoints together to work toward a single objective.
3. **Fostering a product culture:** Establishing a culture that is centered around building the best products that solve customer pain points can be facilitated by leadership without authority. Product managers create an atmosphere where all team members are in agreement with the overall objectives of the product by motivating teams and creating a common vision.
4. **Developing connections and building strong relations:** It is productive to establish sincere connections with stakeholders, colleagues from different departments, and team members. This entails gaining an understanding of people's goals and motivations so that they can be approached based on their preferences. It is also important to have a close relationship with technology and channel partners to ensure product success in the long run.

5. **Encouraging teams:** Much of product managers' responsibility is to motivate teams by highlighting the significance of their contributions and tying their labor to a greater vision. By praising and commemorating group accomplishments, they can foster a productive and upbeat work atmosphere.

6.5 Business Acumen

Technical expertise and leadership qualities are crucial in the ever-changing field of product management, but being business savvy is the key that sets the top 10% of product managers apart from the rest. It is crucial to be able to comprehend, navigate, and match product strategies with more general business goals.[22] Top-notch PMs understand that decisions made on products are not isolated from the routine business's decisions, rather, they are critical to the latter. As a result of this, product managers need to actively develop business skills, realizing that they are dynamic and need ongoing learning and development. In an environment where business success and product success are inextricably linked, becoming a business-conscious expert is not just a means of advancing in the field; it is basically the cornerstone that elevates most product managers to the top.

The two examples below demonstrate how business acumen could revolutionize a product and turn it into a winner.

Elon Musk and Tesla's business vision: Tesla's success is a clear indication of Musk's business-savvy nature. Beyond Tesla's cutting-edge technology, Musk's knowledge of consumer preferences, the auto industry, and the value

---

22. Detroja, P., Mehta, N., Agashe, A. (2020). *Product Management's Sacred Seven: The Skills Required to Crush Product Manager Interviews and be a World-Class PM.* Seattle, Washington: Paravane Ventures.

of sustainable business practices all play a part in Tesla's dominant position in the electric vehicle (EV) market.

Bill Gates's vision of the computer for everyone: In 1975, Bill Gates and Paul Allen founded Microsoft. They understood the power of computers and set the bold vision to have computers on every desk and every home in the world.

6.5.1 The strategic significance of business acumen

1. **Strategic decision-making:** Product managers with business acumen are able to make decisions that are in line with organizational objectives. It is essential to comprehend how decisions about products affect revenue and profitability if you want to promote sustainable growth.
2. **Market dynamics and competition:** Expert product managers have a deep understanding of the competitive landscape and market dynamics. They can evaluate market trends, spot opportunities, and successfully position products thanks to their business acumen.
3. **Financial literacy:** Product managers at the top of their game are adept at interpreting financial reports, comprehending budgetary constraints, and recommending resource-optimization decisions that have the biggest possible impact.
4. **Pricing decision:** Deciding on the most appropriate price for a product is one of the challenging tasks a product manager does. To be considered a top-notch product manager, one has to hone his/her pricing skills and really get good at it over time.
5. **Customer-centric business model:** Experienced product managers create a business model that is focused

on the needs of the customer, making sure that the features of the product meet their needs and offer real value. They understand how user experience affects customer happiness and retention, and how good experiences lead to business success.

6.6 Relationship Management

Technical mastery and strategic vision are critical in the dynamic field of product management, but the secret sauce for becoming one of the top 10% performers is effective relationship management. To promote cooperation, align interests, and achieve success, it is essential to establish and maintain relationships with teams, customers, and stakeholders.[23]

6.6.1 The strategic significance of relationship management

1. **Building trust and rapport:** Cooperation and open communication become easier when effective relationship management cultivates trust and rapport with stakeholders.
2. **Stakeholder alignment:** Having solid relationships with stakeholders helps departments work together to achieve common goals and objectives.
3. **Customer engagement:** Building a rapport with consumers encourages loyalty, obtains insightful input, and improves the customer experience in general, all of which contribute to the success of a product.

---

23. Sandy, K. (2020). *The Influential Product Manager: How to Lead and Launch Successful Technology Products*. Oakland, California: Berrett-Koehler Publishers.

6.7 Negotiation

For product managers, negotiation is the magic that turns an idea into reality. Top-notch product managers are aware that developing connections, lining up interests, and adding value are more important in negotiations than showing dominance. Prospective product managers ought to see negotiation skills as a lifelong learning process, acknowledging their influence on both product and organizational success.

6.7.1 The strategic significance of negotiation

1. **Vendor and partner relations:** When interacting with partners and vendors, negotiation is essential. Contracts, conditions, and alliances are negotiated by product managers to make sure outside partnerships advance the interests of the company and its product.
2. **Allocation of funds and resources:** A product manager's work always involves negotiating funding approvals, project schedules, and resource allocation. The best use of resources for maximum impact is ensured by negotiation mastery.
3. **Getting ready and making plans:** This involves prioritizing learning about the goals and objectives of each party engaged in the negotiation and projecting possible scenarios and results to help product managers be ready for a range of negotiation situations.
4. **Win-win solutions:** Rather than approaching negotiations as a zero-sum game, PMs with negotiation mastery adopt a collaborative approach that looks for solutions that benefit all the parties. PMs need to identify shared goals and areas of agreement as well as disagreements

with other parties to negotiate in such a way that everyone feels that they got a good deal.

5. **Emotional intelligence:** Recognizing and controlling your own emotions as well as those of the other parties in the negotiation is essential in order to keep the atmosphere productive. To lay the groundwork for fruitful negotiations, PMs need to use emotional intelligence to cultivate relationships and trust.

6.8 Attention to Details

While product managers communicate with various organizations and customers on a day-to-day basis, keeping an eye on little details and communicating the points precisely is an important responsibility of the product manager. Lack of attention to detail during the development phase can result in building a product that is not useful for the customers. Similarly, a lack of attention to detail may cause confusion among different departments that can be time-consuming and expensive to fix later on. Even when understanding customer problems and writing PRD, attention to detail is key to ensuring the right feedback is captured and the final product aligns with the product manager's vision.

6.8.1 The strategic significance of attention to detail

1. **Quality assurance:** In order to guarantee the quality of a product, meticulous attention to detail is essential. Carefully examining features, functionalities, and user experiences is necessary to ensure a perfect final product.

2. **Excellence in user experience:** It is crucial to ensure accuracy in design components, user interfaces, and

the overall user experience. Good design meets and even surpasses customer expectations because of meticulous attention to detail.

3. **Extensive recordkeeping:** Product managers should create thorough and precise product requirements that are devoid of any ambiguity. They are also expected to take great care when documenting user stories to ensure that user needs and expectations are well understood.

4. **Better understanding of customer problems:** PMs need to pay attention to detail to comprehensively understand the customer problem as well as the environment in which the product operates. Without that, customers can't build strong customer empathy, resulting in sub-par solutions to customer problems.

6.9 Data Analysis

Analyzing large sets of data is one of the most important skills top-performing product managers have. It is a PM's duty to use data analytics to obtain useful insights into customers' behaviors, preferences, and buying patterns. They can also use information about their products or in-house metrics to gauge their performance in the market. Product managers also need to keep an eye on the product pipeline data and ensure the product is meeting the business target set at the start of the year. Some of the most common analytical tools used by product managers include but are not restricted to:

1. **Tableau:** Known for its user-friendliness, Tableau is a powerful business intelligence and data visualization tool that PMs can use to gain insights about product

usage and it can be shared with the broader teams to influence decisions.

2. **Google Analytics 360 Suite:** Known as a secure and dependable tool, product managers can use Google Analytics 360 suite to gain insights about customer usage and how they interact with the product.

3. **DataDog:** With DataDog, PMs can monitor and analyze an organization's technology stack to ensure applications and services run smoothly.

Apart from using these tools to understand customer behavior, PMs need to keep an eye on product pipeline and other data so that they can use the insights gained from the data to make the right business decisions.

Chapter Summary

- Product managers need to demonstrate genuine empathy towards their organizations' customers. It takes empathy to comprehensively understand the customers' pain points and oversee the development of products that solve customer problems.

- For top-notch product managers, communication remains one of the most effective tools for connecting with all stakeholders to actualize the organization's product vision.

- Having deep knowledge of the applicable technologies and industry-specific/domain expertise is essential for becoming one of the top 10% of product managers.

- Even though they do not normally have power or formal authority over other teams within their organizations, high-performing product managers influence and lead teams and ensure cross-functional alignment.

- Being business savvy—knowing what business decisions to make at the right time to support their activities—can go a long way to streamline everything product managers do while overseeing a product's lifecycle.

- A great product manager must be an amazing negotiator and constantly needs attention to detail. He/she must also have a deep understanding of how to document, analyze, and interpret large amounts of data to make the right business decisions.

Quiz

1. Being able to relate to customers in order to understand their pain points and share their feelings is referred to as…..

   a. Empathy
   b. Technical expertise
   c. Domain knowledge

2. To become one of the top 10 product managers, it is not necessary to demonstrate some level of empathy with customers.

   a. False
   b. True

3. All but one is the primary reason why every product manager must be empathetic with their customers.

   a. To lure them into buying a product
   b. To strengthen the existing customer relationship
   c. To achieve customer-centric product innovation.

4. Which of these is not the purpose of communication in product management?

   a. Stakeholder engagement
   b. Bridging the communication gap
   c. Learning from the competitors

5. Active listening is considered a prerequisite for effective communication.

   a. False
   b. True

6. For communication between product managers and other stakeholders to be well-received and efficient, it must be....
   a. Accurate and detail-oriented
   b. Rude
   c. Misleading

7. When included in their communication, visuals can help product managers convey their messages clearly and understandably.
   a. False
   b. True

8. By properly analyzing large sets of data, product managers can have useful insights into customers' behaviors, preferences, and buying patterns.
   a. False
   b. True

9. One of the merits of "leading without authority" is that a product manager should be able to....
   a. Seamlessly influence decision-making with other teams
   b. Force every stakeholder to do whatever they want
   c. Cause disagreements in other teams he/she doesn't belong to

10. To join the top 10% product manager league, having business acumen is one of the desirable skills or attributes.

   a. True
   b. False

Answers

1 – a	2 – a	3 – a	4 – c	5 – b
6 – a	7 – b	8 – b	9 – a	10 – a

CHAPTER 7
Product Management Specializations

Key Learning Objectives
- Difference between B2B and B2C product management
- General PM vs growth PM vs platform PM
- Inbound vs outbound product management

Just like in the case of engineering where engineers can be software engineers, hardware engineers, AI/ML engineers, product managers also have some specializations. While the goal of the product manager remains the same, which is to build the product that makes customer life easy, the role and responsibility of the PMs vary based on types of the products they are working on, their goals, and whether they are working with the engineering team to build the product or they are mainly focused on creating an awareness for the product. In this chapter, you will learn about different specializations for the product manager role.

7.1 B2B vs. B2C Product Management

While both business-to-business (B2B) and business-to-consumer (B2C) product managers are focused on building the products for their customers, the techniques and strategies to succeed vary slightly based on whether you are working on B2B vs B2C products.

Here are some of the striking differences between B2B and B2C product management:

1. **Understanding the markets:** B2B product management revolves around meeting the complex demands of companies or businesses, whereby products are frequently customized to satisfy particular organizational specifications. On the other hand, B2C product management addresses the varied tastes or preferences of individual customers, requiring products that appeal to a wider consumer market. To ensure the product meets the customer demands, B2B product managers rely on doing the POC and gathering feedback from the customers. Depending upon the customer feedback and traction in the market, they can decide to make the product generally available to all the customers. On the other hand, B2C customers rely on experimentation and A/B testing to monitor whether the feature meets the customer's needs and make iterative changes as necessary.

2. **Complexity and customization:** In business-to-business transactions, there is a high degree of complexity. Products have many features and can be customized in many ways to meet the complex operational requirements and workflows of businesses. These include products such as switches, routers, enterprise security products, etc. B2C products, on the other

hand, typically embrace simplicity and user-friendly interfaces to appeal to a wide range of users. Some good examples of B2C products are WhatsApp, Facebook, and Google. Products like Office365 and Google Drive can be categorized as both B2B and B2C products.

3. **Sales cycles:** The sales cycle in B2B product management is a marathon. To get through organizational hierarchies and close deals, complex negotiations, consultations, checking how the product will fit into existing infrastructure, and relationship-building are required. The B2C sales cycle, on the other hand, is distinguished by its rapidity and is frequently driven by marketing initiatives and impulsive purchases or demographic expectations. In addition, the dollar value of an average B2B deal is comparatively higher than that of B2C.

4. **Relationship building:** B2B product managers make significant investments to cultivate enduring connections with important stakeholders in their client companies/businesses. This means being aware of their problems, matching product offerings to strategic goals, and offering continuous assistance. On the other hand, B2C product management focuses on creating a sense of brand loyalty and communicating unique brand perception that will make them buy the product time and time again.[24]

5. **Complexity of decision-making:** In B2B products, a large number of stakeholders are involved in making the purchasing decision. Each of these stakeholders might have different goals and hence, a B2B product

---

[24]. Haines, S. (2013) The Product Manager's Survival Guide: Everything You Need to Know to Succeed as a Product Manager. New York: McGraw-Hill Education.

manager has to ensure the product appeals to different stakeholders. B2C purchase decision-making, on the other hand, is primarily focused on a few stakeholders at the most, including the end user, and hence, the B2C product manager has to mainly focus on end users, along with other elements such as price, brand perception, ease of use, and user reviews.

6. **Pricing strategies:** Pricing strategies are important in both B2B and B2C product management, though they take different forms in each case. Pricing is frequently negotiated in the B2B sector based on variables like volume discounts, contract terms, and value-added services. Additionally, the final purchase price for the product might vary based on the customers. B2B product managers often bundle different products together to increase the penetration of the product while building a competitive advantage. On the other hand, B2C products are rarely bundled together and the purchase price remains constant across all the customers.

7. **Customer experience and support:** Customer experience (CX) and support are crucial for both B2B and B2C products. Customer support in the business-to-business (B2B) sector is defined by high-touch, personalized interactions that are targeted at solving complicated questions, resolving technical problems, and offering proactive advice to maximize product utilization. To guarantee flawless customer experiences, B2B product managers place a high priority on building strong support infrastructures, which include specialized support teams, technical support hotlines, and self-service portals. On the other hand, B2C customer experiences are frequently characterized by self-service channels, user-friendly

interfaces, and expedited checkout procedures that are designed to reduce obstacles and optimize convenience. Delivering frictionless experiences across various touchpoints, such as websites, mobile apps, social media platforms, and physical retail locations is the main goal of B2C product managers. Both B2B and B2C product managers also use customer feedback methods and data analytics to continuously improve the overall customer experience.

7.2 Generalist PM vs. Growth PM vs. Platform PM

7.2.1 Generalist product management

The processes of creating and overseeing a product from start to finish are included in general product management. A generalist product manager handles all these steps which may include but are not limited to undertaking the market research and analysis, managing the product strategy and planning, executing product development with engineering teams, creating customer-focus messaging and feedback loop, liaising with the sales/marketing team to draft the most appropriate campaigns or marketing for the product, and obtaining feedback from customers for product improvements. The generalist PMs are ultimately responsible for the success of the product including revenue as well as the profit and loss.[25]

---

25. Rugh, S. (2023) The Art of Product Management: Building the Bedrock of Product Success. Spokane, Washington: Jester Labs.

7.2.2 Growth product management

Growth product management involves data analysis, experimentation, and feature implementation targeted at driving key metrics. Growth product management focuses specifically on strategies and tactics to accelerate user acquisition, engagement, retention, and even increasing monetization for the company.

To find growth opportunities and inform decisions, growth product managers mainly rely on data analysis. This entails gathering and examining user data from multiple sources and conducting web analytics, funnel analysis, and user behavior tracking. Growth product managers can spot trends, patterns, and optimization opportunities by analyzing data.

They also test theories and optimize different product aspects, such as feature placements, pricing schemes, and user onboarding flows, through experimentation such as A/B testing and multivariate testing. This entails creating experiments, figuring out what success metrics are, and reviewing the outcomes. Growth product managers can reduce risk, accelerate learning, and promote continuous improvement by conducting iterative experiments.

Growth product managers work closely with marketing teams to carry out growth campaigns and initiatives. This entails matching target audience segments and marketing objectives with product positioning, messaging, and features. They also collaborate with technical teams and data analysts to extract meaning from user data and spot trends and expansion prospects. Growth product managers can create comprehensive growth plans that connect users and produce outcomes by fusing qualitative and quantitative data.

7.2.3 Platform product management

The goal of platform product management is to build the underlying platforms that can be used by internal teams within the company to build the final customer-facing products.

While each product team can build its own functionality independently, building the platform functionality allows teams to reuse the existing functionality, resulting in stable code and reducing the time it takes to launch new products and features to the market.

Figure 7.1 An example product organization supporting multiple products built on top of a set of shared components

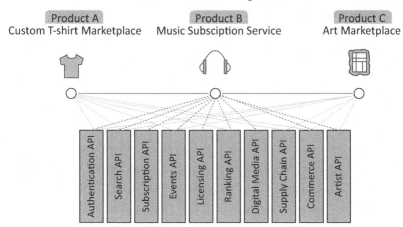

Source: Jenkins, Wyatt. "Making the Shift to Platform Product Management." *Medium* (blog), April 8, 2016. https://medium.com/

In the example shown in Figure 7.1, different products within the organization need some fundamental functionalities such as authentication, licensing, search, event API, etc. Instead of building these functionalities independently, the platform product team can build these functionalities in such a way that they can be reused across all products, resulting in faster time to market.

Considering the product platform touches multiple products across the organization, the platform product managers need to build a scalable and resilient platform that can serve the needs of different products across the organization. Platform product managers need to collaborate closely with individual product managers and should be well-versed in technical concepts such as APIs and system architecture.

7.3 Inbound vs. Outbound Product Management

In some companies, especially startups, a single product manager is responsible for building the right product as well as communicating the value of the product to the end customers. However, in some of the other companies, especially big companies, the product management organization is divided into 2 groups - the inbound product manager is responsible for building the right product and the outbound product manager is responsible for creating the product positioning and creating the awareness of the product. Let's look at the areas of responsibilities for inbound and outbound product managers.

Figure 7.2 The specializations of product managers

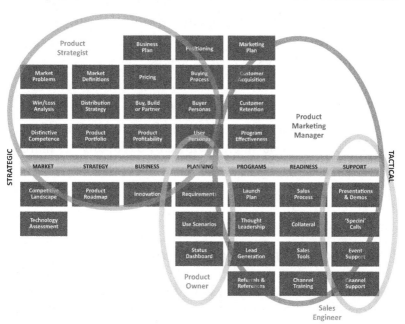

Source: Pragmatic Institute - Resources. "The Strategic Role of Product Management." https://www.pragmaticinstitute.com

7.3.1 Inbound product management

Conducting market analysis, understanding customer pain points, and then collaborating with the engineering team to build a product that meets customer demands are the primary responsibilities of the inbound product manager. Figure 7.2 shows the role of the inbound product manager aligns more with the product strategist. To achieve this goal, an inbound product manager undertakes the following responsibilities:

- Conducting market and competitive analysis and building the long-term strategy and roadmap for the product

- Creating Product Requirements Document (PRD) and collaborating with the engineering and UX/UI team to make sure the right product is built for the end customers
- Conducting POC as well as A/B testing for the product and coming up with a plan to iteratively improve the product
- Ensuring alignment between different teams to make sure all the departments within the company are marching in the same direction
- Defining and tracking Key Performance Metrics (KPI) for the product

7.3.2 Outbound product management

Once the product is built, the outbound product manager is responsible for ensuring the product is positioned correctly and the customer as well as the sales team can educate the customers on product differentiation and value with the goal of creating awareness about the product. The diagram above shows the role of the outbound product manager aligns more with the product marketing manager. Sometimes, an outbound product manager is also responsible for driving POCs (Proof of concepts) for the customers to ensure they are successful.

An outbound product manager is concerned with product marketing, sales enablement, and customer engagement. The outbound product manager works closely with the go-to-market (GTM) team to create awareness about the product. To achieve the goal of creating awareness of the product, an outbound product manager is responsible for handling the following responsibilities:

- Creating the positioning document for the product and educating customers/prospects on the product value as well as differentiation
- Facilitating the go-to-market responsibilities and assisting the sales team in closing the deal
- Driving POC success for the product and ensuring the customer feedback is incorporated into the roadmap
- Facilitating the sales training and channel partner training, and ensuring consistent messaging of the product across all the channels
- Representing the company at tech events to create awareness about the product

7.3.3 Key differences between inbound and outbound product management

1. **Focus:** While an outbound product manager focuses on maximizing the value and success of current products in the market through marketing, sales, and customer engagement, an inbound product manager is primarily concerned with understanding customer needs and market demand to guide product development.
2. **Responsibilities:** Outbound product managers are in charge of product marketing, sales enablement, and customer engagement; inbound product managers, on the other hand, are in charge of product strategy, roadmap planning, and feature prioritization.
3. **Timeline:** An outbound product manager is primarily concerned with post-launch activities like marketing, sales, and customer support, whereas an inbound product manager is usually involved in the early stages of product development, from ideation to launch.

4. **Collaboration:** Outbound product managers work closely with marketing, sales, and customer success teams to market and sell current products, while inbound product managers work closely with engineering, design, and IT teams to develop and deliver new products.

Although inbound and outbound product managers handle different responsibilities, their primary goal is to build the right product and ensure product adoption in the market. As already mentioned, in many organizations, a single product manager handles end-to-end responsibilities of both inbound and outbound product managers and hence, is responsible for the ultimate success of the product.

Chapter Summary

- Like other professions, product management has specializations too.
- B2B product managers focus on building products that cater to big companies that might be building the product for their customers. Conversely, B2C product managers focus on building the products for individual consumers.
- The growth product managers concentrate fundamentally on using data-driven approaches to drive user acquisition, engagement, retention and even increasing monetization for the company.
- The platform product managers focus on building the foundational functionality for the company that can be used by different products within the organization to build the final customer-facing products. Building the platform functionality allows teams to reuse the existing functionality, reducing the time it takes to launch new products and features to the market.
- An inbound product manager collaborates with the product development team to build the right product based on customer preferences and market demands. On the other hand, an outbound product manager oversees product positioning and messaging, sales enablement, and customer engagement with the goal of creating awareness for the product.

Quiz

1. The kind of product management that caters to the needs and requirements of other businesses is called....
   a. B2C product management
   b. B2B product management
   c. Platform product management

2. Which of the following is not expected of a B2B product manager?
   a. Customizing products according to businesses' requirements
   b. Catering for the individual consumer preferences
   c. Engaging in intense, company-wide negotiations

3. True or false? The sales cycle in B2C product management is shorter than in B2B product management's sales cycle.
   a. False
   b. True

4. Which of the factors are not usually associated with B2B product management?
   a. Users' demographics
   b. Complex decision-making process
   c. Product's return on investment (ROI) prioritization

5. When undertaking B2B marketing, which of the following is NOT applicable?
   a. Provision of industry-specific content
   b. Use of case studies
   c. Provision of coupons

6. True or false? It is not necessary for B2B product managers to remain abreast of industry trends, emerging technologies, and changing corporate needs.
   a. True
   b. False

7. True or false? Only B2B product managers should be concerned about regulatory compliance and data privacy, B2C product managers aren't not expected to pay attention to that.
   a. True
   b. False

8. Which of these distinctive features is not associated with the growth product management?
   a. Creating developer tools
   b. Handling data analysis
   c. feature implementation targeted at driving user acquisition metrics.

9. A .... product manager's job entails focusing on building the foundational functionality for the company that can be used by different products within the organization to build the final customer-facing products.
   a. General
   b. Product
   c. Platform

10. Generalist product managers are different from platform product managers because they …..
   a. Oversee a product's entire life cycle
   b. Create platforms and ecosystems to manage their products
   c. Analyze data to discover how to better serve each demographic better

Answers

1 – b	2 – b	3 – b	4 – a	5 – c
6 – b	7 – b	8 – a	9 – c	10 – a

Chapter 8
Commonly Used Product Management Frameworks

Key Learning Objectives
- Practical models and frameworks for product managers
- A thorough breakdown of all the components of each of these frameworks

From time to time, product managers rely on various frameworks to make strategic decisions and consequently measure the successes of their activities at every stage of the product management lifecycle. This chapter critically looks into some frameworks that are commonly used by product managers to carry out their day-to-day duties. Some of these frameworks have been briefly mentioned in different chapters of this book, but they are discussed in great detail in this chapter.

8.1 SWOT Analysis

Figure 8.1 shows the components of the SWOT analysis, which is usually at the center of the company's strategy framework for product managers. SWOT is an acronym for strengths, weaknesses, opportunities, and threats. The questions raised in each of the SWOT analysis boxes in the figure are common ones that product managers always seek to find plausible solutions for.

Figure 8.1   SWOT analysis

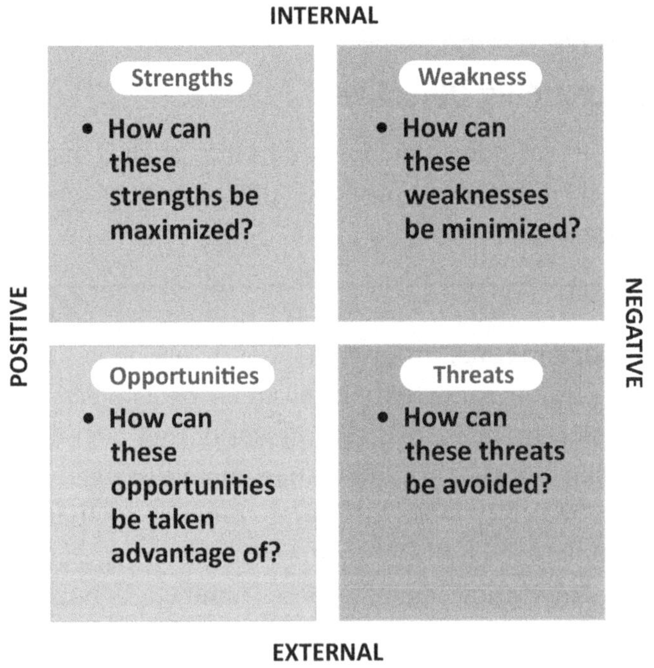

	INTERNAL	
POSITIVE	**Strengths** • How can these strengths be maximized?	**Weakness** • How can these weaknesses be minimized?	**NEGATIVE**
	Opportunities • How can these opportunities be taken advantage of?	**Threats** • How can these threats be avoided?	
	EXTERNAL	

Source: Adapted from "What Is SWOT Analysis?" https://www.visual-paradigm.com

1. **Strengths:** The term strengths refers to internal elements that provide the business with a competitive edge. This could include resources like a well-known brand, cutting-edge technology, or skilled employees. For example, Google has an edge over tech companies

because of so much user information/data. This same thing applies to Facebook, holding information of about 2.09 billion daily active users. Similarly, Amazon and Apple, Inc. rely on their supply chain networks and distribution centers to lead their products or services globally.

2. **Weaknesses:** Weaknesses are internal factors that could impair the competitiveness or performance of the business. These may include things like out-of-date technology, scarce resources, or ineffective procedures.
3. **Opportunities:** Opportunities are external circumstances that the business may take advantage of. This could include new client segments, emerging market trends, or strategic alliances.
4. **Threats:** Threats are external factors that might negatively impact the performance or competitive position of the business. These might include conditions such as increased competition, modifications to regulations, or downturns in the economy.

By utilizing the SWOT analysis, product managers can obtain important insights into the company's market position and formulate plans to leverage strengths, address weaknesses, seize opportunities, and counter threats. In the end, these efforts will help the company achieve its strategic objectives as far as creating a competitive product line is concerned.

8.2 5C Analysis

In product management, knowing the environment in which a business operates is essential. There are five important dimensions of the 5C analysis framework, as shown in Figure 8.2, that can help organizations know their operating environments better.

Figure 8.2 A company's situational (5C) analysis

Company
- Products
- Competitive advantages
- Goals
- Brand

Collaborators
- Partners & Investors
- Suppliers & Distributors
- Service providers
- Content relationships

Customers
- Target audiences
- Customer motivations & Behaviors
- Communication channels
- Customer perceptions

Competitors
- Established & emerging competitors
- Competitor strengths & weaknesses
- Competitor strategies & tactics
- Capability gaps

Climate
- Laws & regulations
- Social & behavioral trends
- Economic trends
- Technologies

Source: Bollig, Maxim. "Situation Analysis in Marketing." *Svaerm Online Marketing Frankfurt* (blog), January 25, 2021. https://svaerm.com

Let's take a look at how to perform the 5C analysis:

1. **Company:** Examine the organization's internal operations, taking note of its resources, culture, and organizational structure. Evaluate the organization's strengths, weaknesses, and capabilities to determine its ability to carry out its plans successfully.

2. **Customers:** Examine consumer behavior and the target market. Recognize their wants, needs, and problems in order to create experiences and products that they will find appealing.

3. **Competitors:** Evaluate competitors' tactics, products, and positioning in the market to establish a unique market position, and pinpoint areas of differentiation and competitive advantages.

4. **Collaborators:** Assess alliances, partnerships, and suppliers that have an impact on the creation and distribution of products. Develop symbiotic partnerships to expand the product's reach and ecosystem.

5. **Context/Climate:** Take into account the industry's broader socioeconomic, technological, and regulatory influences. To stay ahead of the curve and proactively adapt strategies, it is important to anticipate trends, disruptions, and shifts.

8.3 Porter's Five Forces

Product managers use Porter's five forces framework to get thorough insights into their industries' dynamics. They evaluate the attractiveness and intensity of competition by looking at five important factors as shown in Figure 8.3.

Figure 8.3 Porter's five forces

Source: Adapted from Hessing, Ted. "Porter's Five Forces." *Six Sigma Study Guide* (blog), April 25, 2014. https://sixsigmastudyguide.com/porters-five-forces/.

1. **Buyer bargaining power:** This means recognizing the negotiating power that buyers have when it comes to terms and prices. The number of purchases made, the accessibility of alternatives, and the cost of switching from one product to another are all factors to be considered. If buyers refuse to purchase a product, it will definitely fail. Their ability to dictate products' trends and purchasing patterns gives buyers great power. Buyers can exhibit their power in various ways, such as shunning a product, spending their hard-earned money on other alternatives, or returning a product they think doesn't meet their requirements.

2. **Supplier bargaining power:** This stands for determining how much of an impact suppliers have on costs and product quality. This is affected by switching costs, input differentiation, and supplier concentration. In principle, suppliers can decide to change the prices of their products (such as raw materials, software, etc.), modify their products' quality level, and increase or decrease their products' availability. All of these can have a serious impact on a product under development.

3. **Threats of new entrants:** This is all about considering barriers to entry such as capital requirements, economies of scale, and regulatory constraints. Increased barriers lessen the pressure from competitors by discouraging new entrants. In addition, those who are aspiring to enter into a new industry may be discouraged from doing so if the time of entry is inconvenient, other costs like franchise fees, licenses, and buying new equipment are expensive, and there are mandatory legal requirements and other difficult barriers.

4. **Threats of product or service substitution:** This involves identifying substitutes (products or services) that meet similar demands in the market. The demand for an organization's products may be limited by substitutes, and its pricing power can be challenged by the manufacturers of those substitutes. The threat of substitution may be heightened by a number of factors such as the availability of better substitutes, buyer preferences, most especially those motivated by price sensitivity, and the uniqueness of offerings.

5. **Competitive rivalry intensity:** This involves measuring the level of abrasiveness in the industry. The number of competitors, the rate of industry growth, and the degree of product differentiation are important yardsticks to pay serious attention to. Competitors can strategically demonstrate their intrinsic power by bringing innovative products or services to the market, offering better customer experiences, lowering their prices, or optimizing their operational efficiency.

8.4 Cluster Analysis

Cluster analysis, also sometimes referred to as segmentation analysis or taxonomy analysis, is an integral part of the widely used product management frameworks. Cluster analysis is a form of attitudinal research that helps organizations fully understand how customer attitudes affect purchases. When organizations have some idea about what consumers are thinking or believing about certain product categories as well as their specific needs, PMs can use this information to create segments that align with consumer needs and preferences.

Usage studies can be helpful when conducting a cluster analysis. When consumers are asked this important question, "What *do you think or believe about this product category?*" Their answers can be rated on "agreed-disagreed" scales or ratings out of 5, 7, or 10.

Consumer responses will clearly indicate their attitudes behind making some trade-offs to be able to accept the organizations' product categories in question. The differences in attitude between different customers will allow an organization to divide the customers into different segments.

Highlighted below are some ways to do market segmentation based on cluster analysis:

- **User-based segmentation:** This is the simplest form of customer segmentation. It can be a priori segmentation (a user-based segmentation) that is predominated on pre-existing and common observable characteristics seen in consumers. Typical examples are demographic segments based on demographic elements such as age, economic status, education, etc.

- **Usage-based segmentation:** A usage segmentation tends to separate users into either a heavy user/buyer or a light user/buyer, and their levels of usage may be categorized from 1 to 10.

8.4.1 Types of cluster analysis

There are three intrinsic kinds of cluster analysis, namely:

1. **Hierarchical clustering:** This is all about separating data or products into groups according to their similarities, and also finding a means to measure their similarities and differences so that the data can be further narrowed down based on their differences. For

example, for a group named "vehicles", we can expect it to contain "Sedan", "SUV", "Truck", and "Bus". But if we further classify the dataset as a vehicle that can transport 10-20 students to school, then the dataset is narrowed down to only "Bus".
2. **K-clustering:** This refers to the practice of grouping things that are similar into new sets of clusters that may be related. For example, clothes such as "hats", "sweaters", "mufflers", "t-shirts", and "slacks" can be further divided into two different clusters if we use the classifications "winter clothes" and "casual wear".
3. **Two-step clustering:** Some product managers may decide to use a two-step clustering procedure which, in fact, is the combination of both the hierarchical and K-clustering.

Cluster analysis helps product managers to create products that are appealing and useful to the target markets, based on customers' needs, preferences, and behaviors.

8.5 Conjoint Analysis

Product managers can better understand customers' preferences and make well-informed decisions about features and pricing by using conjoint analysis—a framework that combines consumer choice theory and statistical techniques to analyze how customers value different feature attributes within a product or service. Respondents are shown different product profiles with varying levels of each feature, and they are asked to select their favorite option. Product managers can then analyze the utility functions that result from this process to determine how important each feature is and how much of an impact it has on overall preference.

Figure 8.4 Conjoint analysis

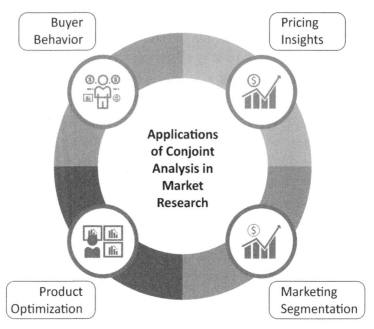

Source: Adapted from Fleetwood, Dan. "How Businesses Can Use Conjoint Analysis for Market Research." *QuestionPro* (blog), July 30, 2019. https://www.questionpro.com

As revealed by Figure 8.4, the conjoint analysis enhanced product managers' market research by providing them with essential information about buyer behavior, market segmentation, product optimization, and pricing insights.

Through the identification of features that customers are willing to pay extra, this framework also helps with pricing strategy optimization. By concentrating on characteristics that add the greatest value for customers, conjoint analysis can contribute to the prioritization of product development efforts. It also makes scenario analysis easier, allowing product managers to model how various product configurations would affect revenue and market share.

Conjoint analysis, in general, gives product managers the ability to make data-driven decisions that correspond with consumer preferences, resulting in more successful product launches and increased market penetration while competing with the other products in the market.

Figure 8.5 An example of conjoint analysis

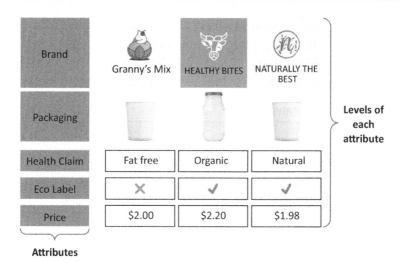

Source: Conjointly. "Conjoint Analysis 101: With Example for NPD - Conjointly." https://conjointly.com

Figure 8.5 reveals different brands, their packaging types, prices, health claims, and whether they have eco-labeling or not. By applying conjoint analysis, businesses can:

- Choose desirable product features for new or refined products
- Discover buyers' willingness to pay for certain features compared to other features
- Determine the best pricing option for their products
- Test buyers' adoption potential for new products or services

- Determine how packaging, product claims, and advertising messaging can make a difference in a product's lifetime

8.6 4P Analysis

Once the engineering team starts building the product, product managers are expected to work closely with the product marketing team to draw up a go-to-market (GTM) plan to bring the product to the market. The 4P analysis helps with exactly that.

Figure 8.6 4P analysis

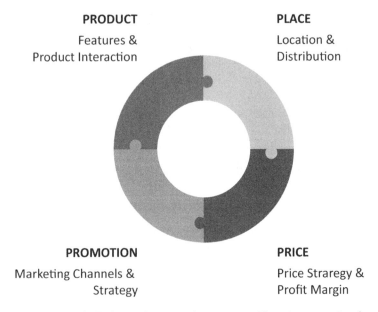

Source: Pratt, Micah. "What Is the 4P Marketing Matrix?" Business.org, October 11, 2022. https://www.business.org

As shown in Figure 8.6, the 4Ps is an acronym for product, price, place, and promotion, the four essential elements of the marketing framework.

- **Product:** The most important aspect of any marketing strategy is the product itself. It must be developed in such a way that it fulfills customer requirements and possesses a design and features that can help solve customers' pain points.[26]
- **Price:** Product managers need to take multiple factors into consideration while deciding the price for their products. It is sensible to consider the competitors' pricing, value-based pricing, and the cost incurred in building the product while deciding the price for the product in the market.
- **Place:** To reach the target markets and consumers, product managers must take advantage of the expanded distribution networks, utilizing a wide range of sales channels. By making their products available and accessible to a target customer at the right place, PMs can increase their revenue and market share.
- **Promotion:** Product managers can raise awareness about their products and stimulate increased patronage or sales among their targeted customer bases. This involves conducting GTM activities as well as working with the marketing team on planning and running well-coordinated campaigns or promotions, across different media, that will eventually turn prospects into loyal ambassadors of the products.

---

26. Kersten, M. (2018). *Project to Product: How to Survive and Thrive in the Age of Digital Disruption with the Flow Framework*. Sebastopol, California: IT Revolution Press.

8.7 Customer Purchases Decision Framework

The AIDA model, as discussed in Chapter Four, is a well-known model adopted among product managers and marketers to track consumer buying behaviors from awareness to interest, decision, and then action.

Figure 8.7 The AIDA model

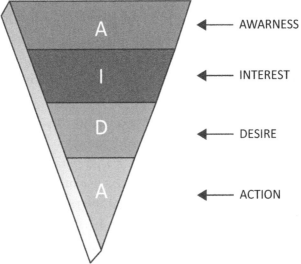

Source: Hanlon, Annmarie. "The AIDA Model and How to Apply It in the Real World - Examples and Tips." Smart Insights, March 20, 2023. https://www.smartinsights.com

1. **Awareness:** Before a product can be purchased, consumers must learn about it through marketing initiatives, word-of-mouth, or other sources.
2. **Interest:** After learning about a product, buyers become curious about it; this curiosity is frequently triggered by its features, the pain points it can solve, and other special selling points. During the interest

stage, the customer starts evaluating potential products that can solve their problem and narrow down their choices.

3. **Desire:** Customers evaluate a product's suitability or usefulness at this point by contrasting it with alternatives and taking into account attributes like cost, quality, and user feedback. They will express the desire to purchase the product at this junction.

4. **Action:** Customers will move ahead with making a purchasing decision after discovering some positive and useful attributes of the product they have finally selected. On most occasions, their decisions are influenced by the product's competitive cost, features, ease of use, functionality, and brand trust.

8.8 Business Model Canvas

Carrying out an all-encompassing market research is one of product managers' routine responsibilities. The business model canvas serves as a helpful framework for them to better understand some significant elements of their businesses.

Figure 8.8 Business model canvas

KEY PARTNERS	KEY ACTIVITIES	VALUE PROPOSITIONS	CUSTOMER RELATIONSHIPS	CUSTOMER SEGMENTS
Who are our key partners? Who are our key suppliers? Which key resources are we acquiring from our partners? Which key activities do partners perform?	What key activities do our value propositions require? Our distribution channels? Customer relationships? Revenue streams?	What value do we deliver to the customer? Which one of our customers' problems are we helping to solve? What bundles of products and services are we offering to each segment? Which customer needs are we satisfying? What is the minimum viable product?	How do we get, keep, and grow customers? Which customer relationships have we established? How are they integrated with the rest of our business model? How costly are they?	For whom are we creating value? Who are our most important customers? What are the customer archetypes?
	KEY RESOURCES		**CHANNELS**	
	What key resources do our value propositions require? Our distribution channels? Customer relationships? Revenue streams?		Through which channels do our customer segments want to be reached? How do other companies reach them now? Which ones work best? Which ones are most cost-efficient? How are we integrating them with customer routines?	

COST STRUCTURE	REVENUE STREAMS
What are the most important costs inherent to our business model? Which key resources are most expensive? Which key activities are most expensive?	What value are our customers willing to pay? How much do they currently pay? What is the revenue model? What are the pricing tactics?

Source: *Harvard Business Review*. "A Better Way to Think About Your Business Model." May 6, 2013. https://hbr.org/2013/05/a-better-way-to-think-about-yo.

Figure 8.7 shows the various components of a business model canvas. Let's look at how to use a business model canvas in detail.

1. **Key players:** This involves identifying the key partners/suppliers and the motivation for the partnerships.
2. **Key activities:** This step involves highlighting the key activities a company performs to build the product and create differentiation in the market. What are the most important activities required to streamline customer relationships, distribution, revenue stream, etc.?
3. **Key resources:** What are the most important resources at the disposal of the company? This could include employees, product distribution, supply chain advantages, and so on.
4. **Value propositions:** This entails describing the value customers stand to gain from interacting with the company, and how the company's product aims to eliminate customers' pain points.
5. **Customer relationships:** What kinds of relationships do the customers expect from the company - Is it a 1:1 relationship or is it a self-serve model? And how can such relationships be affordably and efficiently integrated into the company's existing business operations?
6. **Customer segments:** Which categories of customers is the company creating value for? Which are the company's most important customer segments?
7. **Channels:** What are the most cost-effective and efficient distribution channels, and how do customers prefer to be reached?
8. **Cost structure:** This involves identifying the cost structure of a company's business operations and learning how much the key activities will cost. It is also essential to highlight the available resources.
9. **Revenue streams:** What value are the customers willing to pay for? What are their preferred payment methods?

And what is their frequency of payment? How much revenue are we generating from different product lines and different regions where we are selling the product? What is the current revenue model and what pricing tactics can we leverage?

8.8.1 Key Takeaways

- The business model canvas allows product managers and other senior managers to visualize the most important aspects of their business. Hence, it is heavily used in startups as well as big companies.
- A business model canvas allows businesses to understand how different elements of the business or product interact with each other.
- It allows product managers and entrepreneurs to easily analyze and communicate their strategy with various stakeholders.

Business model canvas has also been discussed in detail in Chapter Two.

8.9 PESTLE Analysis

The PESTLE analysis provides an organized method for evaluating the external macro-environmental elements influencing a company and its business activities. It also allows the companies to identify new markets or countries that would be conducive to expanding the business operations and increasing revenue in the long run. By undertaking a detailed analysis of political, economic, social, technological, legal, and environmental factors, product managers can better understand the market environment, spot new opportunities, and reduce risks by thoroughly examining these variables. A well-executed PESTLE Analysis will reveal the extent to which these factors can influence the organization's business activities.

Figure 8.9 The PESTLE analysis

Political	**E**conomic	**S**ocial
• Political Stability • Corruption • Foreign Trade Policy • Tax Policy • Funding Grants	• Economic Growth • Interest Rates • Inflation • Disposable Income of Consumers • Labour Costs	• Population Growth • Age Distribution • Cultural Barriers • Consumer Views • Workforce Trends
Technological	**L**egal	**E**nvironmental
• Emerging Technologies • Maturing Technologies • Copyright and Patents • Production and Distribution • Research and Investment	• Regulation • Employment Laws • Consumer Protection Laws • Tax Policies • Anti-trust Laws	• Climate • Environmental Policies • Availability of Inputs • Corporate Social Responsibility

Source: "Business Theory Analysis: PESTLE - ABLE Activator," November 24, 2021. https://activator.bg

The elements of PESTLE analysis are highlighted below:

- **Political factors:** There are some political factors that may affect an organization's day-to-day operations. These may include political stability, corruption, foreign trade policy, tax policy, funding grants, etc.
- **Economic factors:** Companies are undoubtedly affected by the prevailing economic situations in the jurisdiction

where they are operating. If there is measurable economic growth, little inflation, and increasing disposable incomes, consumers will be willing to spend their hard-earned money on buying products/services from the companies making them. However, when there are high interest rates and the labor cost is expensive, the products in the market may be more expensive than usual, and consumers may choose to buy less than expected.

- **Social factors:** Social factors such as population growth, consumer views, age distribution, workforce trends, and cultural barriers may promote or threaten a company's aspiration to become successful.

- **Technological factors:** An organization requires new and existing technologies to run every aspect of its business operations. Depending on how technologically advanced the market is, the company can decide whether it would be profitable to introduce the product in the long run. A simple example of this would be a need for consistent availability of electricity and high-speed internet to run the software company. Similarly, it is advisable to undertake regular research and identify new opportunities for investment and product distribution.

- **Legal factors:** Organizations are expected to play by the rules and regulations of the locations where they are situated. It is equally essential to observe all the laws relating to taxes, employment, human rights, privacy, antitrust, and consumer protection.

- **Environmental factors:** An organization's operations may be affected by some environmental factors such as climate, environmental policies, corporate social responsibility policies, etc. Carrying out a well-organized PESTLE analysis can reveal any or all environmental problems that may affect the organization's operations.

8.10 BCG Growth Market Share Matrix

As shown in Figure 8.10, the Boston Consulting Group (BCG) Growth Share Matrix is an extensively used framework in product management for examining a company's portfolio of products or its business units.

Figure 8.10 BCG growth market share matrix

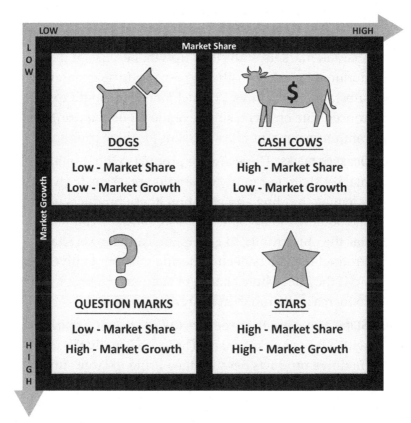

Source: Adapted from "BCG Matrix", Management Consulted, https://managementconsulted.com

It was created by the Boston Consulting Group and divides products into four groups according to their relative market share and rate of growth.

1. **Dogs:** These are low-market-share products in markets with slow growth. Usually, these products don't make a lot of money and sometimes even lose money. Product managers ought to think about selling off or discontinuing these items unless they have a strategic value, like enhancing other offerings.
2. **Cash cows:** These are the products with a large market share in markets with slow growth. Because of their dominant market position, these products generate substantial cash flow. Product managers ought to concentrate on increasing revenue while requiring the minimum amount of investment for these products.
3. **Question marks:** These are the products with a small market share in rapidly expanding markets. If given adequate funding and attention, these products have the potential to become successful and the company has the opportunity to gain significant market share. Product managers need to decide whether to give them up if they have little chance of success or invest in them to increase their market share.
4. **Stars:** These are the products in fast-growing markets with a large market share. These are usually the most lucrative products because they bring in large sums of money in the fast-growing markets. To keep up its current growth trajectory, the company needs to invest substantial money to further expand the market and fend off the competitors as much as possible.

8.11 Pricing Decisions

Product managers are always involved in making pricing decisions. This requires careful analysis of multiple pricing options and frameworks to identify the best possible pricing structure for a product or service. A pricing-based market analysis is a process of gathering extensive information about consumer needs, preferences, and customers' willingness to pay for products and services. Product managers also need to take competitors' pricing into consideration before finalizing the pricing for the product. Following are a few pricing strategies that PMs can use:

1. **Cost-based pricing:** This entails analyzing every expense related to product development, manufacturing, marketing, and distribution, together with any other costs like overhead and operating costs, which are considered to be fixed and variable costs before coming up with the price of the product.

2. **Value-based pricing:** This involves outlining the product's distinct value proposition and making price decisions in relation to consumers' perceptions of that value. It is imperative for product managers to figure out the main merits and characteristics of their products and what sets them apart from rivals' offerings while evaluating the most appropriate pricing structures for their products.

3. **Competitors pricing:** This involves understanding how much your competitors are charging for a similar product and pricing your product in that range. The final price of the product could be higher or lower than that of competitors based on whether the market perceives you as a high-end premium product or a low-cost provider.

Even after the pricing is decided, product managers need to keep an eye on competitors' activities, market dynamics, and consumer input in order to modify pricing strategies as necessary. Finding areas for optimization and improvement entails analyzing sales data, profitability metrics, and customer satisfaction over a long period of time.

8.11.1 Software pricing models

Figure 8.11 describes some of the commonly used pricing models for software products.

Figure 8.11 Software pricing models

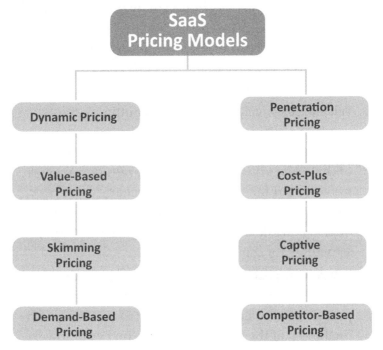

Source: "SaaS Pricing Strategy Can Make Or Break Your Business." https://scalecrush.io

1. **Penetration pricing:** This refers to the practice whereby an organization strategically enters into a very competitive market by intentionally lowering its prices against those of its rivals to gain some adoption among consumers.
2. **Dynamic pricing:** SaaS companies, for instance, adopt dynamic pricing strategies to stay competitive while scaling their businesses. They update their prices, increasing or decreasing them while considering some important factors such as customer demand, market trends, and competitor pricing. Examples of dynamic pricing include value-based pricing, competitor-based pricing, time-based pricing, and demand-based pricing.
3. **Usage-based pricing:** This is also referred to as consumption-based pricing. It entails charging users based on how much they utilize the product.
4. **Concurrent or simultaneous user pricing:** This pricing model allows a limited number of users to use the same product at the same time. If more than a fixed number of users log into the software at a time, there may be additional fees, or the application won't work. A common example would be Netflix limiting how many users can use the same account simultaneously.
5. **Flat rate pricing (a type of captive pricing):** In this approach, a product/service is given a fixed price irrespective of how many times it is used or how long it takes to complete (if it is a service). Other examples of captive pricing include pay-as-you-go and tiered pricing.
6. **Per-user pricing:** As its name implies, this pricing is based on how many users are using the product. If

there are ten people using the product, they have to pay ten times per user billing.

7. **Annual pricing:** This entails that the users have to pay the price for using the product for the entire year. In certain cases, the price may increase after some years. A common example would be Amazon charging their Prime customers every year so that they can use Amazon Prime benefits for the full year.

8. **Feature pricing:** This is an example of tiered pricing whereby a company offers different prices for the same product based on which features and functionalities customers like to use. In freemium models, the customer can use the baseline version of the product for free by signing up for the product. However, if they want to use the additional features or capabilities, they will have to pay for them. The common example would be that signing in to use LinkedIn is free but if you would like to use additional features and send more InMail, you need to purchase a LinkedIn premium subscription. Another example would be using Gmail for consumers is free but if you need extra storage capabilities, you need to pay extra money for the storage.

9. **Cost-plus pricing:** This involves estimating the business expenses/costs of creating a product, and adding a certain markup percentage on that to determine how much the product should be sold.

10. **Skimming pricing:** This is a pricing strategy that is sometimes adopted by some SaaS companies whereby they choose to steadily lower their products' prices as competition against their products increases. This approach is also referred to as price skimming.

8.11.2 CLV, price discrimination, elasticity

Product managers usually examine and leverage the interrelationship among customer lifetime value (CLV), price discrimination, and elasticity when deciding on a product's price, as described below[27]:

1. **Customer Lifetime Value (CLV):** In order to make sure that net revenue from each customer exceeds the cost of acquisition and retention, pricing decisions are guided by an understanding of the long-term value of customers.
2. **Price discrimination:** Revenue can be optimized without alienating any specific group by customizing prices based on customer segments or their willingness to pay. Organizations can offer the same product or service to various clients at varying prices according to their different purchasing capabilities. In principle, there are three types of price discrimination that organizations use to sell their products/services to their customers:

    - **First-degree price discrimination**—In this case, the organization charges different prices for different customers even though they might be using the same product. An example would be airlines charging different customers different prices for similar seats.
    - **Second-degree price discrimination**—This refers to a practice whereby organizations allow their customers to choose special deals or sales if they fulfill the conditions for the deals. For example, buy-two-get-one-free deals.

---

[27]. LeMay, M. (2022) *Product Management in Practice: A Practical, Tactical Guide for Your First Day and Every Day After.* Sebastopol, California: O' Reilly Media.

- **Third-degree discrimination**—This occurs when special discounts are given to members of certain groups, such as students, senior citizens, etc.

3. **Elasticity:** Determining price elasticity helps in estimating how variations in price can impact demand. Product managers may optimize revenue and market share by modifying pricing strategies in accordance with the degree to which customers are responsive to price changes.

It must be stated that effective pricing strategies necessitate ongoing evaluation and adjustment in response to changes in the market, competitors' pricing, and consumer preferences. To ensure the long-term growth and success of their products or services, product managers must carefully balance profitability, competitiveness, and customer satisfaction while gauging how much to price their offerings.

Figure 8.12 Elastic demand curve

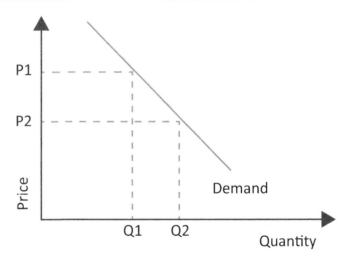

Source: Adapted from "Elasticity of Demand | Ag Decision Maker." Accessed February 19, 2025. https://www.extension.iastate.edu

8.12 Build, Partner, Buy Analysis

Product managers use the build, partner, buy analysis framework to decide whether to build the product internally, partner with a third-party vendor, or buy the company to improve the market penetration for the product.

The build option is about determining whether the organization has the capability required to internally develop a product. This may encompass factors like the accessibility of resources, proficiency, lead time, and compatibility with the existing strategic goals. Product managers may also consider the viability and economics of developing the product from scratch as well as the time required to gain additional market share after launching the new product.

The partner option requires exploring possible partnerships with external entities, including vendors, other companies, and open-source communities. This choice may have benefits like taking advantage of complementary skills, breaking into untapped markets, or quickening development processes through pooled resources. Product managers need to assess possible partners' suitability, taking into account aspects such as goal alignment, dependability, and possible risks.

The buy option entails determining whether to outrightly purchase another company and then, considering merging the acquired product to the existing portfolio of the products. To guarantee compatibility with the current systems and ensure long-term strategic fit, product managers need to perform extensive due diligence and understand the possible financial implications of the action. It is also essential to consider how the newly acquired products will integrate with the organization's current product line.

8.13 Pragmatic Marketing Framework

Figure 8.13 Pragmatic marketing

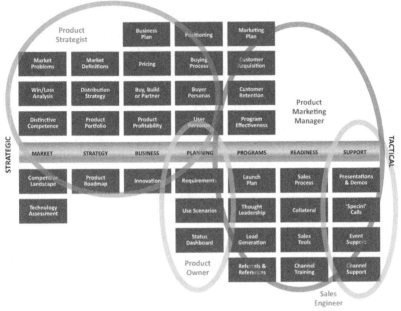

Source: Pragmatic Institute - Resources. "The Strategic Role of Product Management." https://www.pragmaticinstitute.com

The pragmatic marketing framework showcases the responsibilities that product managers need to undertake to build and launch products to the market. To achieve this goal, the product manager needs to work cross-functionally with other departments. A pragmatic marketing framework enables PMs to understand the roles and responsibilities they need to undertake to succeed as a PM. The roles and responsibilities, as highlighted in earlier chapters as well, are elaborated in Figure 8.13.

Each box covered in the pragmatic marketing framework covers responsibilities and activities needed to be performed to bring the product to the market. While product managers in the early stage of start-ups handle all these responsibilities on their own, product managers in established firms work cross-functionality with different functions including product marketing manager, product owner, corporate strategy, and sales engineers, along with the engineering team to bring the product to the market.

The pragmatic marketing framework allows organizations to ensure all the bases are covered to significantly improve the chances of launching a successful product.

8.14 TAM/SAM/SOM Analysis

Figure 8.14 TAM, SAM, and SOM

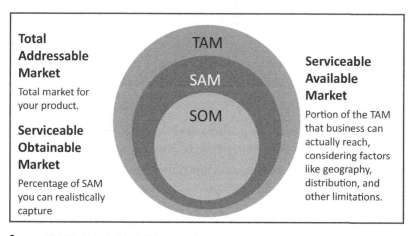

Source: "TAM, SAM & SOM: What Do They Mean & How Do You Calculate Them?," June 21, 2024. https://blog.hubspot.com

Product managers utilize the TAM, SAM, and SOM analyses to identify the market potential or the size of the consumer segment and estimate what percent of the market can be targeted and realistically gained by launching the product.

- **Total addressable market (TAM):** This is the total potential market for your product or service, without considering any limitations. It represents the maximum revenue opportunity if you could capture 100% of the market.
- **Serviceable addressable market (SAM):** SAM focuses primarily on the particular segment of TAM that the product managers expect to target. While deciding the target segment for the product, PMs need to consider the size of each segment and then identify the market that they can serve. For instance, in the US, the SAM for computer keyboards (a segment of computer accessories) is estimated at $1.4 billion (2024).
- **Serviceable obtainable market (SOM):** This refers to a section of SAM that a business has the capability to successfully capture. This involves taking into account factors such as competition, limited resources, market penetration, and geography in which the product operates.

Using the insights from their TAM, SAM, and SOM analyses, product managers can discover opportunities for growth, strategically enhance their go-to-market approaches, and identify market saturation.

8.15 Kano Model

Figure 8.15 Kano Model

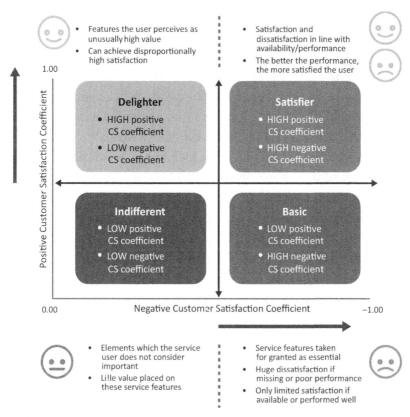

Source: Sapio Research. "Kano Analysis | Understanding Customer Needs With Kano." Accessed February 19, 2025. https://sapioresearch.com

As already discussed in section 3.2 (under feature prioritization), product managers use the Kano Model as a framework during feature prioritization. This framework allows product managers to divide the features into must-have, good-to-have, and features that will be delightful or indifferent to the customers. It divides features into five emotional response types, which are explained below:

- **Must-be (or must-have) features:** These are the basic features that are expected to be parts of a product. Consumers will feel dissatisfied if these basic features are not present in the product. Imagine an iPhone without a camera and Bluetooth capability! That may trigger iPhone lovers to be angry with Apple, Inc. and may consider switching to other smartphones.

- **Performance features:** These are features that consumers hope to enjoy while using the product because they probably improve their personal or professional lives. For example, an Instagram vlogger whose iPhone doesn't have a camera may feel truly dissatisfied because they need the camera to record their vlogging activities.

- **Attractive features:** Attractive features add extra excitement to a product or give consumers some level of delight. They can be used to differentiate one product from another. However, their absence may not decrease the consumer's satisfaction with the product.

- **Indifferent features:** These are features that consumers are indifferent to; they don't necessarily consider it good or bad to have or not have them.

- **Reverse features:** Some features that are not generally desirable to most consumers but which, if absent, may cause a certain consumer segment to feel dissatisfied with the product. For example, a large percentage of iPhone users may not, in principle, care about asking "Siri" questions. However, very techy iPhone users will feel seriously dissatisfied if their version of the iPhone doesn't have "Siri".

By using the Kano Model, product managers can identify and prioritize the features that provide the greatest value to customers while efficiently utilizing available resources.

8.16 Sample PRD Format

A product manager builds a PRD to clarify the requirements so that the engineering team can build a product that is consistent with customer requirements. The product manager needs to write crisp requirements that are clearly understood by different stakeholders, including engineering, design, and IT teams. While different organizations have their own format for PRD, here is one of the sample formats for the PRD.

Figure 8.16 Sample PRD format

Product requirements

Product name:	
Vision	Where you want the product to be in the future
Description	Brief overview of what your product does and for whom
Timing	When you plan to ship the new customer experience
Status	NOT STARTED / ON TRACK / AT RISK
Team	Product manager, development team, designers, QA, etc.
Background	competive landscape, user interviews, and other research
Strategic Alignment	Business case, including goals for your product and any supporting initiatives
Metrics	How product performance will be measured
Who it Benefits	Who will benefit from the product — link to any personas you have
Use Cases	Step-by-step descriptio of different scenarios in which a users might use your product to solve specific challenges
Assumptions	Hypothesis behind how your solutions will solve the customer's problem, along with technical feasibility
Investment Required	Budget, headcount, and other resources
Product Architecture and Components	Funclonal elements of the product and how they relate to one another
Core Features	Discrete areas of functionality that deliver value to users. You can then break them down further using the epic and feature templates below.
User Experience (UX) and User Interface (UI)	How the user will interact with the product and how the interfaces will look and behave

Source: "Product Requirements Document (PRD): Best Templates for PMs." Accessed February 19, 2025. https://www.aha.io

Product managers can use the Sample Product Requirements Document (PRD) format as a starting point to describe the features, functionalities, and vision of their products. Usually, it has the following main sections:

1. **Title and introduction:** Clearly state the name of the product/feature
2. **Objectives:** Specifies the precise aims and goals that the product is intended to accomplish. This could include acquiring early customers and reaching the target revenue goal within the stipulated time frame.
3. **Problem statement:** Clearly state what problems customers are facing today and what problem are we trying to solve by building this new product/feature.
4. **Acceptance criteria:** Cover different scenarios of the new product or a feature and how is the product expected to behave under these different scenarios.
5. **Features:** Lists the essential features and functionality of the product, arranged in order of importance for users and business requirements.
6. **Functional requirements:** Describes the specific functions and behaviors of the product; wireframes or mockups are frequently included for clarity.
7. **Non-functional requirements:** The term "non-functional requirements" refers to requirements that are crucial to the success of the product but may not directly relate to its core functions. Examples of these requirements include performance, security, scalability, and compliance.
8. **Dependencies:** This section identifies any external limitations or dependencies that could affect the product's development or introduction.

9. **Timeline and milestones:** This contains important deliverables and milestones as well as the suggested schedule for releasing the early version and the GA version of the product.
10. **Approval:** Provides stakeholders a chance to examine and give their approval to the document, ensuring that it is in line with product direction.
11. **Metrics and success criteria:** Specifies the metrics and key performance indicators (KPIs) that will be used to measure the product's effectiveness and success after launch. User engagement, retention rates, conversion rates, and income generation are a few examples of success metrics.

Chapter Summary

- The 5C analysis gives product managers the unique opportunity to fully understand the environment in which their organization operates, while Porter's five forces give them the chance to analyze their industry dynamics.
- The SWOT analysis reveals useful information about an organization, including its strengths, weaknesses, opportunities, and threats.
- With cluster analysis, product managers can assemble comparable data points while segmenting the market whereas conjoint analysis combines consumer choice theory and statistical techniques to analyze how customers value different feature attributes within a product or service
- 4P analysis is a useful marketing tool that many product managers utilize to bring products to the market.
- Product managers usually use the customer purchase decision framework as a tool for understanding consumer buying behavior.
- PESTLE analysis helps product managers understand the macro-environment affecting the business today and in the future. It also allows product managers to evaluate new markets for the business.
- Boston Consulting Group (BCG) Growth Share Matrix is an extensively used framework in product management for determining an organization's portfolio of products and their relative market share as well as identifying growth areas.
- Making pricing decisions remains one of the most important tasks product managers undertake.
- Product managers use the build, partner, buy analysis framework to decide whether their organizations should

partner with outside organizations, acquire pre-existing products, or develop a new product internally to expand market share.

- The pragmatic marketing framework provides a comprehensive view of product managers' roles and responsibilities they need to undertake to succeed as a PM.
- TAM/SAM/SOM analysis allows product managers to identify the size of the market and assess how much market share they can realistically target and capture with the product.

Quiz

1. Which of these is not connected with the 5C analysis?
   a. Company
   b. Capital
   c. Competitors

2. Product managers use the 5C analysis to understand their organizations' operating…
   a. Environment
   b. Funding
   c. Location

3. Product managers employ Porter's five forces to understand their organizations' market dynamics.
   a. True
   b. False

4. Which of these is NOT one of the barriers to new entry that organizations often face when exploring a new market?
   a. Economies of scale
   b. Capital requirements
   c. Product name

5. The "O" in SWOT analysis means…..
   a. Openness
   b. Opportunities
   c. Operations

6. In SWOT analysis, the "weaknesses" are internal factors that could impair the competitiveness or performance of the business.
   a. False
   b. True

7. ...... is the process of assembling comparable objects or data points according to specific, common features or attributes.
   a. Kano Model
   b. Cluster analysis
   c. Porter's five forces

8. When customers are given a discounted pricing option that offers them some deals when they meet certain conditions such as the *"buy-two-get-one-free"* promotion is an example of....
   a. First-degree price discrimination
   b. Second-degree price discrimination
   c. Third-degree price discrimination

9. Product managers usually utilize 4P analysis in their marketing drive. Which of these statements is not correct?
   a. P= Price
   b. P=Problem
   c. P=Product

10. The first phase in the customer purchases decision framework is…..
    a. Evaluation
    b. Awareness
    c. Interest

Answers

| 1 – b | 2 – a | 3 – a | 4 – c | 5 – b |
| 6 – b | 7 – b | 8 – b | 9 – b | 10 – b |

CHAPTER 9
How to Get Into Product Management

Key Learning Objectives
- Transitioning from different roles to PM
- Key hard and soft skills for PMs
- Cracking the PM interview
- Career paths and the relevance of MBA in product management

How do I get into product management is one of the most common questions aspiring product managers have, whether they are college students or professionals who are currently performing other roles but planning to transition into product management. This chapter provides some useful and practical information that anyone seeking to become a product manager can find very helpful.

9.1 Transitioning From Different Roles to the PM Role

Product management is a vibrant, multidimensional industry that draws professionals or experts from various backgrounds looking to have a significant strategic impact. Making the move from other roles to product management calls for a combination of skills, educational background, and personal readiness. Here are some steps to help you transition to the product manager role:

1. **Recognize the functions of the product manager role you are interested in:** Successful product launches are driven by the vision, development, and efforts of product managers. Their duties cover a broad range of activities as discussed earlier. So, if anyone is desirous of transitioning from their current jobs or professions to PM, they need to, first of all, identify which specific PM responsibilities(s) they can take up in the current role. This will facilitate their switching to a PM role comparatively easily. Note that the skills don't have to be an exact match but as long as they are transferable to the PM responsibilities, that should suffice. Also, please note that when you are starting as a PM or applying for the entry-level product manager role, you don't need to have all the skills and may not have handled all the responsibilities mentioned in pragmatic marketing covered in Chapter Eight.

2. **Evaluate your existing skills and experience:** Determine which of your current role's skills are transferable in order to become a product manager. Product managers benefit from having abilities like project management, data analysis, customer interaction, and strategic thinking.

3. **Fill the skill gap:** To improve the skills that are currently missing from your repertoire, enroll in classes or work toward certifications. Courses in data analytics, UX/UI design, and product management basics are available online through sites like Coursera, Udemy, and LinkedIn Learning. Another way to gain some of these skills is to do side projects that can be added to your resume later.

4. **Network within the industry:** Make connections in the industry by attending product management-related conferences, meetups, and events. Through networking, you can find job opportunities, establish connections with possible mentors, and gain insights into the field.

5. **Seek internal opportunity:** Look into product-related projects and roles within your current organization, if at all possible. Inform the appropriate stakeholders of your desire to transition into product management and ask for mentorship from existing product managers.

6. **Develop a strong portfolio:** A well-designed portfolio allows you to highlight your abilities and expertise. Provide case studies of the projects you've worked on, emphasizing the results and contributions you've made. Stress your capacity to solve issues and produce results.

7. **Gain hands-on experience:** To acquire practical experience, volunteer for side projects. This could entail helping with product launches, performing user research, or working with product teams on feature improvements.

8. **Personalize your cover letter and resume:** Emphasize experiences and abilities that are pertinent to product management in your cover letter and resume to show

how you made an impact in previous roles. Use metrics and accomplishments.

9. **Consider an entry-level position:** If required, be willing to begin in product roles that are entry-level or in positions that are related, like associate product manager or associate product manager. These positions can lead to more senior positions in the future and offer valuable experience to learn your craft.

10. **Continuously learn and adapt:** Since the field of product management is always changing, make a commitment to lifelong learning by reading books, and blogs, listening to podcasts, and taking online courses to stay current on market trends, new technology, and best practices. Have a growth mentality and be open to new chances and challenges.

11. **Develop effective communication skills:** Product management success depends on having effective communication skills. Develop your capacity for clear communication, persuasion, and cooperation with cross-functional teams. Seek feedback and engage in active listening to continuously enhance your communication abilities.

12. **Develop relationships across functions/departments:** Product managers communicate with engineers, designers, marketers, and sales representatives, among other departments. Develop close bonds with coworkers in all of these roles to promote cooperation and alignment toward shared objectives. Recognize their viewpoints and make use of their experience to advance the success of your product.

13. **Become data-driven:** Information is vital to the decision-making process in product management. Learn about data analysis tools and methods such as user analytics,

A/B testing, and market research. Utilize data to evaluate features, set priorities for features, and assess the success of product initiatives.

14. **Specific industry knowledge:** As a product manager, one of the most important responsibilities is to understand the market of the product as well as different players in the market to come up with a strategy that will differentiate the product from others. Someone who want to transition to the PM role will surely have a strong advantage if they have a decent understanding of the industry they operate in, along with different players in the space.

9.2 Hiring and Interview Process

Product management is a dynamic field that calls for a special set of abilities that include technical proficiency, business savvy, and a thorough understanding of user needs. Getting hired and cracking the interview process is necessary to land a job in product management. Here's how to ace the PM interview:

1. **Understand the role:** It's essential to understand the function of a product manager before beginning the interview process. As you already know, product managers are in charge of overseeing a product's development from conception to launch to completion. They prioritize features, work with cross-functional teams, and make sure the product satisfies business and customer needs. So, keep in mind that interview questions may require you to demonstrate your knowledge about all the functions product managers carry out in their organizations. Since there are different PM roles, which have already been mentioned

in previous chapters, it is advisable that the person preparing for a PM interview knows exactly which PM role he/she is going to play if hired.

2. **Prepare your resume:** Make sure that the accomplishments and relevant experiences on your resume highlight your potential for success in a product management position. Highlight your results-driven approach, leadership abilities, collaboration tendency, and strategic-thinking skills. Where it's possible, include metrics and measurable accomplishments to demonstrate your impact.

3. **Research the company:** Before the interview, thoroughly research the company and its products. Understand their market position, target audience, and competitive landscape. Familiarize yourself with any recent news or developments that may impact the company's strategy or priorities. It is equally important for the PM job candidates to understand the product they will be working on; It will be great to, if asked, talk about creative ways they can improve it in order to stand out in the interview.

4. **Prepare for behavioral interviews—STAR Technique:** Behavioral interview questions are used in product management interviews to assess your adaptability to changing circumstances and your capacity for problem-solving based on prior experiences. These questions frequently center on situations you would face in the position, like setting feature priorities, settling disputes among stakeholders, or dealing with unforeseen project setbacks.

An organized strategy for responding to these inquiries is provided by the STAR technique.[28] The Situation, Task, Action, and Result components of your response can help you explain your situation and solution in a clear and succinct manner. First, explain the situation or context in which the problem appeared. Next, describe the task or objective that you need to achieve. Then, describe the specific actions you followed to resolve the issue, along with any strategies or decisions you had to make. It is equally important to underline the impact of your efforts and any lessons gained by presenting the result or outcome of your actions.n Using the STAR approach can help you present your ideas and experiences in an engaging way, which makes it easier for interviewers to evaluate your problem-solving abilities and fit for the product management position.

5. **Master product management concepts:** Prepare to talk about basic product management concepts like agile development principles, market analysis, the product life cycle, popular frameworks used by PMs, and user research techniques. It is also essential to mention elements of pragmatic marketing such as integrating efficient marketing processes into the product life cycle, researching and paying serious attention to customers' preferences, and creating and maintaining marketing channels that promote the product's great benefits to consumers.

6. **Develop problem-solving skills:** Product managers are naturally good at solving problems. Prepare yourself for case interviews where you will be asked to suggest solutions for real-world scenarios. Pay attention to

---

28. Boston Consulting Group (2018). STAR-technique: a how-to guide. https://media-publications.bcg.com/BCG-STAR-Technique.pdf

your capacity for creativity, critical thought, and setting priorities among conflicting interests.

7. **Showcase your communication skills:** Product managers need to communicate clearly because they work with a variety of stakeholders and have to explain complicated concepts. Develop your ability to express yourself succinctly and clearly, whether you're explaining something orally or in written materials like roadmaps or product briefs.

8. **Highlight leadership abilities:** Product managers frequently act as team leaders, fostering motivation, vision, and alignment. Talk about previous instances where you successfully oversaw projects, influenced stakeholders, and provided team mentoring to demonstrate your leadership skills.

9. **Prepare for technical questions:** Product managers should have a fundamental understanding of technical concepts related to product development, even though they are not required to be software engineers. Prepare for technical questions concerning platforms, data analytics, APIs, and other relevant topics. Also, as a PM, it is imperative to spend time with engineers and customers who might be technical. So, having some idea about technical things to make the right recommendations/decisions as and when needed is desirable.

10. **Asking thoughtful questions:** It is likely that you will have a chance to ask additional questions at the conclusion of the interview. Take advantage of this opportunity to show that you are interested in the business and learn more about the role and dynamics of the team. Make meaningful inquiries that demonstrate your analytical reasoning and curiosity.

9.3 Career Paths in Product Management

The different roles product managers play and their diverse specializations have already been discussed in this book. While position titles vary from company to company, here is the general career path for product managers to rise from the entry-level role to the leadership role as a VP or Chief Product Officer (CPO).[29]

Figure 9.1 Product manager's career path

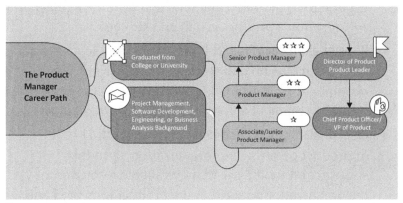

Source: Manager, The Product, and Paul Lopusushinsky. "A Guide To The Product Manager Career Path + Roles And Skills." The Product Manager, September 15, 2021. https://theproductmanager.com

- **Product management intern:** Product management interns work with in-house product managers in the organizations they are doing their internships. Their duties range from learning the basics of product management to assisting product managers with research and simple assignments and equipping

---

29. Haines, S. (2013) *The Product Manager's Survival Guide: Everything You Need to Know to Succeed as a Product Manager.* New York: McGraw-Hill Education.

themselves with the much-needed skills to become fully trained PMs.

- **Associate/Junior product manager:** This is the entry-level PM position. A junior PM assists the in-house product managers in all they are assigned to do.
- **Product manager:** These are fully trained, certified, and experienced product managers. The years of experience may vary from one PM to another.
- **Senior product manager:** This PM has been on the job for several years and may have acquired many experiences leading, managing, and actualizing his/her organization's product vision and strategy.
- **Director of product/Product leader:** A product leader owns the product vision and strategy for the product or portfolio of products. They also have direct reports and could be responsible for multiple products/platforms.
- **Chief product officer/Vice-President of product:** The VP of product owns his/her organization's product strategy and mobilizes all the available resources in the organization to see that the product is created and successfully marketed to the customers who want it. There could be multiple directors/managers reporting to the VP of product, especially in big companies.

9.4 Do You Need An MBA to Become A Successful PM?

An MBA is usually not required, although an MBA might be helpful for acquiring fundamental business-specific skills and other relevant skills required to become a successful product manager. A wide range of backgrounds, including engineering, design, and even liberal arts, are represented among the effective PMs. Apart from fundamental business knowledge, an MBA can also provide plenty of networking opportunities. In the end, it comes down to your objectives and the particular demands of the positions you're aiming for.

As you are already aware, based on the facts presented in this book, product management is a multidimensional profession that calls for a wide range of skills, such as market analysis, user empathy, strategic thinking, and effective communication. There are other ways to succeed in product management outside of earning an MBA, even though an MBA can offer a strong foundation in business concepts and management strategies.

For people who plan to use an MBA to get into a product management role, an MBA in product management and entrepreneurship has become a popular choice because of its extensive curriculum covering a wide range of business topics. A typical MBA program incorporates topics including organizational behavior, marketing, finance, negotiation, and operations to give students a comprehensive understanding of how firms run. For product managers, who frequently have to work with cross-functional teams and make decisions that affect several business elements, this extensive knowledge source is definitely helpful.

Furthermore, case studies, group projects, and internships are frequently incorporated into MBA programs to enable students to apply real-world ideas to practical settings.[30] Aspiring product managers can benefit greatly from this real-world experience since it sharpens their problem-solving abilities and teaches them how to handle challenging business situations.

---

30. McDowell, G.L., Bavaro, J. (2013) *Cracking the PM Interview: How to Land a Product Manager Job in Technology.* California: CareerCup.

Developing a solid professional network is another benefit of earning an MBA in product management. Students attending business schools come from a variety of industries and backgrounds, which fosters a vibrant networking and collaborative environment. MBA students can increase their professional networks and learn from seasoned industry professionals by engaging with classmates, alumni, and faculty members.

Chapter Summary

- People can get into product management either as entry-level job candidates or transitioning from their current professions into becoming product managers. Whichever way, they have to go through a similar PM hiring and interview process.
- To clear a PM interview, some preparation is essential, including drafting a skill-revealing resume, and cover letter.
- While it is not usually a prerequisite to have an MBA to secure a PM job, an MBA can surely provide fundamental knowledge of different fields including marketing, business, strategy, finance, and economics that is extremely useful to succeed as a PM.

Quiz

1. It is usually impossible to transition from another profession into a product management position.
   a. True
   b. False

2. While preparing one's resume for a PM job, it is important to .....
   a. Tell a lie in the resume
   b. Show past accomplishments
   c. Fake some past experiences

3. Why is it always advisable to research an organization before applying to become a PM there?
   a. To discover the CEO's personality
   b. To understand the organization's vision, business model, and products
   c. To find some faults about the organization's existing products

4. What can an aspiring product manager gain from having an MBA?
   a. Knowledge of finance, marketing, organizational management, etc.
   b. Acquire some technical skills, including programming and software development skills
   c. Discover how to undertake engineering tasks in PM

5. It is compulsory to have an MBA before one can become a product manager.
   a. True
   b. False

6. Studying for an MBA is a waste of resources because there is nothing a PM can gain from it.
   a. False
   b. True

7. It is also possible for product managers to become CEOs of their organizations.
   a. False
   b. True

8. Which rank is considered an entry-level position in the product management field?
   a. Director of product
   b. Associate product manager
   c. Product management intern

9. Nowadays, product managers come from all disciplines, such as engineering, sciences, marketing, business administration, etc.
   a. False
   b. True

10. What does the "T" in STAR stand for?
    a. Test
    b. Tasks
    c. Trial

Answers

1 – b	2 – b	3 – b	4 – a	5 – b
6 – a	7 – b	8 – b	9 – b	10 – b

CHAPTER 10
Cracking the PM Interview: Types of Questions and Tips

Key Learning Objectives
- PM requirements of top tech companies
- Types of interview questions and tips to answer them
- The importance of networking and mentorship

A lot of helpful information about the responsibilities, prestige, and benefits of being a product manager has already been covered in the preceding chapters of this book. However, the first hurdle on the way for anyone aspiring to become a product manager is clearing the product manager interviews. This section delves into the nature of product manager's interviews, providing useful examples of PM question types and highlighting the necessary preparations to successfully clear the PM interviews.

10.1 What Tech Companies Look for in PM - Amazon, Microsoft, Apple, and Facebook

Before we move to the various interview questions asked for a PM role, let us look at the job requirements of top tech companies such as Amazon, Microsoft, Apple, and Facebook. This section highlights the key skills they look for in their PMs. If you are looking for a job in a top company, this section will give you insights into what you really need to prepare for.

1. **Amazon:** According to the information provided on the Amazon job portal as of 2025, the company prefers to have a product manager with the following traits, experiences, and skills.

   - **"Knowledgeable:** PMs have a deep understanding of the product's purpose, target audience, and market.
   - **Data-driven:** PMs use data and analytics to make decisions and improve performance.
   - **Results-driven:** PMs focus on delivering high-quality results that meet or exceed expectations.
   - **User-centric:** PMs place a strong emphasis on understanding and meeting user needs.
   - **Adaptable:** PMs can adapt to quickly changing market conditions, technologies, and priorities."[31]

2. **Microsoft:** "Product Managers (PMs) (should) drive development and build consensus throughout the entire product lifecycle. PMs typically apply their background in technology and business domains to define features and

---

[31] amazon.jobs. "Product Manager Interview Prep." Accessed February 18, 2025. https://www.amazon.jobs/content/en/how-we-hire/product-manager-interview-prep.

achieve product vision from product definition and planning through development, release, and end of life."[32]

3. **Apple, Inc.**: *"At Apple, we combine product management/development and product marketing responsibilities into a single, cross-functional Product Management role that collaborates with design, engineering, finance, legal, marketing communications, public relations, market research, sales and support for maximum impact across the organization."*[33]

4. **Facebook:** *"A product manager is a visionary who guides new product ideas from an initial concept to a full-blown product launch. Along the way, we collaborate with world-class engineers and designers to maximize each product's impact on the world."*[34]

5. **Google:** *"Google's approach prioritizes user needs, data-driven decisions, rapid iteration, and collaborative development to build products. By adopting these principles, businesses can foster innovation, improve development speeds, and achieve growth."*. Here are the key Principles of Google's Product Management Approach:

- **Focus on the user:** *Prioritize user needs and understand their goals and pain points.*
- **Be data-driven:** *Use data and analytics to make informed decisions.*
- **Iterate quickly:** *Build and test prototypes, gather feedback, and improve products.*

---

32. "Product Manager - Microsoft Leap." Accessed February 18, 2025. https://leap.microsoft.com
33. "Product Manager, New Products - Careers at Apple," October 26, 2024. https://jobs.apple.com
34. "Product Manager Responsibilities." https://www.metacareers.com/jobs/1345581559397442/

- **Collaborate effectively:** Foster teamwork and cross-functional alignment in product development.[35]

10.2 Types of Interview Questions

Now that you know what top companies look for, let us look at the various types of questions asked during product management interviews:[36]

10.2.1 Product design and improvement questions

These kinds of PM interview questions will assess your knowledge and competence in product design and improvement. It also tests the ability to better understand and communicate customer segments, their pain points, feature prioritization, and the ability to come up with innovative solutions to the problem. Here are some examples:

1. How would you design a consumer application for an online library?
2. Design a product for doctors to fight viruses.
3. How would you improve our product's existing features?
4. Design Netflix for grandparents (Objective: to increase engagement time)
5. How would you improve our existing product line?

---

35. Google Cloud Blog. "Google's Product Management Approach." Accessed June 30, 2025. https://cloud.google.com

36. Lin, L.C., Lu, T. (2017) *The Product Manager Interview: 164 Actual Questions and Answers.* Seattle, Washington: Impact Interview.

> **Tips for answering design and product improvement questions:**
>
> - Identify the user segment you want to target and understand the user and business goals before coming up with features.
> - List down the important pain points of the target persona and identify the most important pain points that are worth solving.
> - Come up with a few features/solutions that can solve customers' pain points and recommend one of the solutions.
> - If time permits during the interview, come up with the UX mock-up for the feature and elaborate on how you will take the product to the market.
> - End the answer with how you will measure the success of the newly released feature and provide a summary. The success metrics could be improvements in user satisfaction, engagement, retention, or an increase in the revenue for the product.

10.2.2 Product strategy questions

Product Strategy questions test your ability to make long-term strategy and growth plans for the product or the portfolio of the products. For this type of question, the candidate is expected to explain the analysis they will conduct using the frameworks covered in Chapter Eight to come up with the right strategy for the product. Examples of product strategy questions include:

1. *What are the biggest threats to Facebook and what can we do to defend against the threats?*

2. Should Amazon expand to more countries in Africa and if so, which countries will be favorable for the entry?
3. Should Google consider entering into the CyberSecurity industry? If so, how should they enter the Cybersecurity market?

Tips for answering product strategy questions questions:

- Understand the frameworks covered in Chapter Eight and identify the frameworks that are relevant to the question at hand.
- Understand both internal and external factors relevant to the company and industry.
- Understand the customer behavior and preferences in the market/region you are targeting.
- Come up with a long-term strategy and provide insights into how we can achieve this goal.
- Identify how you will measure success in the short and long term and summarize the recommendation.

10.2.3 Estimation questions

PM interviewers usually use estimation questions to test the job candidate's problem-solving and critical-thinking skills.[37] It also tests your ability to break down larger problems into small chunks to come up with a solution. Examples of PM estimation questions include:

1. What is the market size for wireless speakers in the US?

---

[37]. McDowell, G.L., Bavaro, J. (2013) *Cracking the PM Interview: How to Land a Product Manager Job in Technology.* California: CareerCup.

2. How many tennis balls can fit in the Boeing 747 airplane?
3. What will be the size of the driverless car market in 2040?

Tips for answering estimation questions:

- Present the scope of the problem.
- Break down the problem using available facts and mathematical assumptions.
- Clarify assumptions with the interviewer and based on the assumption, come up with the approximate answer for the problem.
- Summarize the assumption and the final answer and explain how this will change depending upon the change in assumption.

10.2.4 Behavioral questions

The behavioral questions are designed to check whether the candidate is a good culture fit for an organization. It also helps to understand how the candidate has handled difficult situations and conflicts in the past so that the hiring manager can understand whether the candidate will be able to handle the responsibilities if he/she joins the organization. Some information about the behavioral interview and how to use the STAR framework has already been provided in Chapter Nine of this book. Here are examples of PM behavioral questions:

1. *Walk me through a complex problem you recently solved. What was the problem, and how did you overcome it?*

2. *Tell me the time when you came up with an innovative solution to complex problems.*
3. *Tell me the time when you worked cross-functionally to ensure a product's success.*
4. *Tell me about a time when you had to make a decision without sufficient data.*
5. *Tell me about a time you had a conflict at work and how you resolved it.*

Tips for answering behavioral questions:

Use the STAR framework as discussed before to answer behavioral questions.

- **Situation:** First explain what the situation was. Use real-world experiences and connect them to the question.
- **Task:** Describe your particular role in the situation and enumerate your responsibilities.
- **Action:** Explain what did you exactly do to resolve the issue/problem step by step.
- **Result:** What was the outcome of the action and what did you learn from it?

10.2.5 Measuring success questions (also known as analytical questions)

It is important for PM interviewers to know if a potential PM job candidate truly understands how to measure the success and evaluate the trade-offs. Measuring success interview questions are actually designed to discover if the PM job candidate understands and knows how to interpret large amounts of data and most importantly, understand the key insights and key performance indices (KPIs) from the data. Examples of measuring success PM questions are:

1. *How would you measure the success of the newly built product or feature?*
2. *How do you determine the success of the Instagram Shopping feature?*
3. *As a product manager at Meta, how do you determine the success of Facebook videos?*
4. *As a product manager at Meta, how do you determine why are Facebook friend requests dropping by 10%?*
5. *As a product manager at Meta, what is the north-star metric for Facebook marketplace?*

Tips for answering measuring success questions:

- Explain the feature goals as well as the overall goal for the product under discussion.
- Explain how the customer journey is influenced by the feature.
- Connect customer journey with their behaviors/patterns and quantify their experience with well-defined metrics.
- Explain A/B tests or other experiments you plan to run to better understand customer behavior.
- Identify multiple metrics that can be used to measure success and explain the pros and cons of each approach.
- Identify one of the metrics as the north star metric and provide the summary of the solution.

10.2.6 Technical and coding questions

While product managers are not expected to code during the interview in most companies, interviewers will ask some fundamental technical questions to evaluate the candidate on the technical concepts and ability to have deeper discussions with the engineering teams and evaluate trade-offs. Technical skills are even more important when the product manager is building the product for the technical audience (for example - developer tools) since without technical skills, it will be difficult for the product manager to have customer empathy.

Examples of PM technical and coding questions include:

1. *What happens after you type the URL in the browser?*
2. *Describe the high-level architecture of the current product you are working on.*
3. *What are the most important considerations for increasing the loading speed of the e-commerce website and reducing latency?*
4. *How will you explain cloud computing to your grandmother?*
5. *How can we incorporate artificial intelligence and deep learning to existing and new products?*

Tips for answering technical and coding questions:

- Learn about the fundamentals and protocols that might be relevant for the role you are applying for or those that are widely used in the industry.
- Highlight the technical experience and how it relates to the products that you will be working on.
- Simplify the concepts such that they can be easily understood by non-technical people as well.

10.3 Importance of Networking and Mentorship

Some helpful information has been provided in Chapter Nine of this book about the significance of networking and mentorship for product managers. This section will highlight what to look for when networking or seeking mentors in the field.

- **Experience matters a lot:** Network or receive mentorship from professionals who already have in-depth experience in the skills you are trying to develop. If someone has made a similar transition that you plan to make (for example: from engineering to product management), that person can provide strong guidance on how to bridge the skills gaps to transition to the new role.

- **A recommendation is helpful, too:** Ask for the recommendations from colleagues and associates so that you can quickly find the right mentors. It is also advisable to connect with product management professionals on LinkedIn and other related platforms to find people who have taken similar journeys and gain appropriate guidance.

- **Pay it forward:** While you are learning the best approaches to advance your PM career, do not hesitate to pay it forward. Share your new ideas with colleagues or subordinates who might need them. You know, we learn more from teaching others!

Chapter Summary

- Tech giants such as Apple, Google, Facebook, Amazon, Microsoft etc. look for specific skills in their product managers. While applying and interviewing for the companies, it is important to highlight the skills that are relevant for the specific company and the role.
- There are different types of PM interview questions, such as product design and improvements, case questions, estimation questions, behavioral questions, measuring success, and technical and coding.
- While networking and mentorship are significant in product management, choose your associates and mentors wisely.

Quiz

1. *"Walk me through a complex problem you recently solved. What was the problem and how did you overcome it?"* is an example of a …..question.
   a. Estimation
   b. Behavioral
   c. Technical/coding

2. It is usually NOT important that a PM must have comprehensive business knowledge.
   a. False
   b. True

3. Which of these PM activities is not part of market research and analysis?
   a. Understanding customers' needs
   b. Market segmentation
   c. Handling workplace pressure

4. Why is it necessary to prioritize product features?
   a. To give consumers the most important features first and ensure customer success
   b. To ask consumers to pay a hidden fee later for the best features
   c. To deceive into buying a useless product

5. Which of these statements is NOT technically correct?
   a. All technical PM interviews require all interviewees to code
   b. Not all technical PM interviews ask interviewees to code
   c. Some interviewees may be asked to complete a code during their technical PM interviews

6. "*How would you determine the number of coffee shops in Tokyo?*" is a typical example of a PM ……..question.
   a. Technical
   b. Estimation
   c. Behavioral

7. In principle, it is essential for a product manager to have analytical skills.
   a. False
   b. True

8. Which of these is not one of the tips for passing a PM behavioral interview?
   a. Present a similar situation you have experienced in the past
   b. Be vague in your answer
   c. Describe the steps taken to solve the problem

9. What is the primary purpose of technical/coding questions?
   a. To know if the interviewee has the technical understanding to work with the engineering team
   b. To discover if the interviewee can act under pressure
   c. To understand if the interviewee has some analytic ability

10. Connecting customer journeys with their behaviors/patterns and quantifying their experience with well-defined metrics is a useful tip for answering PM... questions.
    a. Behavioral
    b. Technical and coding
    c. Measuring success

Answers

1 – b	2 – a	3 – c	4 – a	5 – a
6 – b	7 – b	8 – b	9 – a	10 – c

Bibliography

1. Amazon.jobs. "Product Manager Interview Prep." Accessed February 18, 2025. https://www.amazon.jobs/content/en/how-we-hire/product-manager-interview-prep.
2. Bland, D.J. Osterwalder, A. (2019). Testing Business Ideas: A Field Guide for Rapid Experimentation. London: Wiley, p. 34.
3. Boston Consulting Group (2018). STAR-technique: a how-to guide. https://media-publications.bcg.com/BCG-STAR-Technique.pdf
4. Detroja, P., Mehta, N., Agashe, A. (2020). Product Management's Sacred Seven: The Skills Required to Crush Product Manager Interviews and be a World-Class PM. Seattle, Washington: Paravane Ventures.
5. "Consumer Behavior Statistics You Should Know in 2024 [New Data]." Accessed November 29, 2024. https://blog.hubspot.com
6. Fard, Adam. "10 Best Product Vision Statement Examples That Actually Work (And Why)." Adamfard. December 6, 2024. https://adamfard.com/blog/10-best-product-vision-statement-examples
7. Faridani, A. (2021). Why Businesses Can't Afford to Skip Market Research. Forbes, retrieved from https://www.forbes.com
8. GRIN tech. "Geoffrey Moore Positioning Statement with Examples," April 8, 2019. https://the.gt/geoffrey-moore-positioning-statement/
9. Haines, S. (2013) The Product Manager's Survival Guide: Everything You Need to Know to Succeed as a Product Manager. New York: McGraw-Hill Education.
10. Hypothesis. 2024. In Merriam-Webster.com Retrieved February 5, 2024, from https://www.merriam-webster.com
11. Kersten, M. (2018). Project to Product: How to Survive and Thrive in the Age of Digital Disruption with the Flow Framework. Sebastopol, California: IT Revolution Press.
12. Kumar, V. (2008). Customer Lifetime Value: The Path to Profitability. Norwell, Massachusetts.
13. LeMay, M. (2017). Product Management in Practice: A Real-World Guide to the Key Connective Role of the 21st Century. Sebastopol, CA: O'Reilly Media, p. 55.
14. LeMay, M. (2017). Product Management in Practice: A Real-World Guide to the Key Connective Role of the 21st Century. Sebastopol, CA: O'Reilly Media, 65.
15. LeMay, M. (2022) Product Management in Practice: A Practical, Tactical Guide for Your First Day and Every Day After. Sebastopol, California: O' Reilly Media.

16. Lin, L.C., Lu, T. (2017) The Product Manager Interview: 164 Actual Questions and Answers. Seattle, Washington: Impact Interview.
17. Lombardo, C.T., McCarthy, B., Ryan, E., Connors, M. (2017). Product Roadmaps Relaunched: How to Set Direction while Embracing Uncertainty. Sebastopol, CA: O'Reilly Media, 44.
18. Lombardo, C.T., McCarthy, B., Ryan, E., Connors, M. (2017). Product Roadmaps Relaunched: How to Set Direction while Embracing Uncertainty. Sebastopol, CA: O'Reilly Media, 44.
19. Markey, R., Reichheld, F., Dullweber, A. (2009). Closing the Customer Feedback Loop. Harvard Business Review. Available at: https://hbr.org/2009/12/closing-the-customer-feedback-loop Accessed 5 March 2024.
20. Massachusetts Institute of Technology (2024). Why 95% of new products miss the mark (and how yours can avoid the same fate). Retrieved from https://professionalprograms.mit.edu
21. McDowell, G.L., Bavaro, J. (2013) Cracking the PM Interview: How to Land a Product Manager Job in Technology. California: CareerCup.
22. Miller, D. (2017). Building a StoryBrand: Clarify Your Message So Customers Will Listen. New York, HarperCollins.
23. "Product Manager - Microsoft Leap." Accessed February 18, 2025. https://leap.microsoft.com
24. "Product Manager, New Products - Careers at Apple," October 26, 2024. https://jobs.apple.com
25. "Product Manager Responsibilities." https://www.metacareers.com/jobs/1345581559397442/
26. ProductPlan. "RICE Scoring Model." https://www.productplan.com/glossary/rice-scoring-model/.
27. Rollworks (2024). MQL vs. SQL: A Guide to Maximizing Revenue Growth. Available at: https://www.rollworks.com
28. Rugh, S. (2023) The Art of Product Management: Building the Bedrock of Product Success. Spokane, Washington: Jester Labs.
29. Sandy, K. (2020). The Influential Product Manager. Oakland, California: Berrett-Koehler Publishers.
30. Sekaran S. (2020). Product Marketing, Simplified: A Customer-Centric Approach to Take a Product to Market. (Seattle: Amazon, 2020), 32-44.
31. Turayhi S.,. The Launch: A Product Marketer's Guide: 50 Key Questions & Lessons for A Successful Launch. (Seattle: Amazon, 2021), 28-60

Further Learning

Reference Books

1. **The Product Book:** How to Become a Great Product Manager by Carlos González de Villaumbrosia & Josh Anon
2. **Crossing the Chasm:** Marketing and Selling Disruptive Products to Mainstream Customers by Geoffrey A. Moore
3. **Cracking the PM Interview:** How to Land a Product Manager Job in Technology by Gayle Laakmann McDowell & Jackie Bavaro
4. **Inspired:** How to Create Tech Products That Customers Love by Marty Cagan
5. **The Lean Product Playbook:** How to Innovate with Minimum Viable Products and Rapid Customer Feedback by Dan Olsen
6. PM Interview Questions by Lewis Lin
7. **Sprint:** How to Solve Big Problems and Test New Ideas in Just Five Days by Jake Knapp
8. **Launch:** The Roadmap to Product Management Success by Scott D. Anthony
9. **Ship It:** Silicon Valley Product Managers Reveal All by Richard Banfield, Martin Eriksson & Nate Walkingshaw
10. **Product Roadmaps Relaunched:** How to Set Direction While Embracing Uncertainty by C. Todd Lombardo, Bruce McCarthy, Evan Ryan & Michael Connors
11. **Business Model Generation:** A Handbook for Visionaries, Game Changers, and Challengers by Alexander Osterwalder & Yves Pigneur

Made in United States
Orlando, FL
18 September 2025